EVERYBODY'S GOT BEARS

Bravely Facing Down Stress, Anxiety, and Depression to Find an Abundant Life in Christ

DAVID EDWARD CUMMINGS

Dear Laura,
May the Lord bless you
and keep you!
Jn 16:33

Dave Cummings

PRAISE FOR EVERYBODY'S GOT BEARS

"I highly recommend *Everybody's Got Bears* as an insightful resource for gaining a fresh understanding of the potential, sometimes invisible, stressors of a too-busy life. Dr. Cummings' personal journey provides reflective lessons, insights, and strategies for health and hope. Every reader desiring to develop a better life-balance will benefit by taking to heart these strategies for examining your life, slowing down, building resilience, and deepening your faith."

  –BOB BROWER, President of Point Loma Nazarene University

"If you have ever experienced stress, anxiety, or depression – and who hasn't? – you will be greatly helped with this book. Dave Cummings writes from his first-hand experience with authenticity and hope. This is definitely a book I will pass out to others and I know it will be helpful."

  –JIM BURNS, President of HomeWord and award-winning author of *The Purity Code*

"Love it! A really great read that combines refreshing entertainment and deep insight. With his willingness to openly share what most people hide – the persistent struggles that can lead to breakdown – Dave Cummings gives us the ability to breathe, to exhale, to relax in the knowledge that stressors, like bears, can come into anybody's camp. His unique perspective affords us the ability to identify personally with Dave's stories and his journey on the path of balance, healing in Christ, and realizing that you are not alone!"

  –KEVIN MANNOIA, Chaplain of Azusa Pacific University and author of *15 Characteristics of Effective Pastors*

"I have listened to Dave speak many times. He is engaging, funny and very informative. This book reads the same. Dave is very open and honest about the many pitfalls he faced on the road to healing.

His story is so down to earth that most people with overwhelming stress, anxiety and
depression will be able to relate. He applies biblical truth throughout this book. I think the truths that he highlights will bring many people hope and help."

−KATHY MORATTO, Director of Counseling Ministries, Emmanuel Faith Community
Church, Escondido, CA

"Who even has time to read about stress, anxiety, overwork, and fighting bears? Read the first few pages of this book and ask that question again. You do. It will help you unlock that prison you're living in, and set you on a path of the spirit-filled, joyful life you were meant to live. With personal vulnerability and solid research, David Cummings is a knowing and trustworthy guide."

−DEAN NELSON, Director of the Journalism Program at Point Loma Nazarene University
and author of *God Hides in Plain Sight*

"As a Christ follower and tenured biology professor, Dave brings a fresh, creative, and scientifically informed perspective to mental health issues. His message is deeply needed in today's world and today's church. His voice merges practical life experience and biblical understanding that encourages the soul toward next steps of transformation."

−PHIL HERRINGTON, Lead Pastor of Pathways Community Church, Santee, CA

"I'm pleased to enthusiastically endorse Dave Cummings' book *Everybody's Got Bears*. Written from the heart of someone who's struggled, it's an intensely personal tale of his battle with debilitating anxiety and depression. Dave's point-of-view account of his fears and thoughts during his recovery will surely resonate with anyone facing similar challenges. It's a great story of a changed life, moving from heartbreak to hope. I unreservedly recommend it!"

    –MIKE MARINO, popular speaker and author of *Freedom from Anxiety and Depression*

"This book's topic is challenging. The thoughtful, engaging message Cummings unpacks is profoundly optimistic. As I read I found out about the science behind the human mental state. More than that, I learned about myself and how to understand my own emotional experiences. I felt more normal, more human, more hopeful. I am grateful for the wisdom on these pages."

    –DAVE BRUNO, Vice President of Marketing at Lipscomb University and author of *The 100 Thing Challenge*

"Christians struggling with mental health challenges too often remain alone, stuck and confused in the darkness of taboo. Dave Cummings brings light and hope, with a remarkable combination of personal experience, disciplined thought, Christian anchoring, and warm prose. His own story of being toppled from life success by anxiety sets him up to learn the constellation of resources available to those seeking recovery. What he has learned, he shares. For sufferers and those who love them, he gently replaces the twin errors of despair and fantasies of quick-fixes with solid steps forward in grace-filled healing."

    –ROB BARRETT, Director of Forums and Scholarship at The Colossian Forum

This book is not intended to replace professional advice from a licensed therapist or doctor. The author disclaims liability for the application of any of the contents herein. The reader is advised to consult a medical or psychiatric professional regarding treatment of mental and physical health disorders.

Scriptures taken from the Holy Bible, New International Version®, NIV®. Copyright © 1973, 1978, 1984, 2011 by Biblica, Inc.™ Used by permission of Zondervan. All rights reserved worldwide. www.zondervan.com The "NIV" and "New International Version" are trademarks registered in the United States Patent and Trademark Office by Biblica, Inc.™

Names of people and other details may have been changed to protect the identities and privacy of others.

ISBN: 9781092513098

Cover designed by Aimee Cummings (on Instagram @seed.arts)
Pawprints designed by Sydney Cummings (on Instagram @sydxdraws)
Author photos by Drew Renaud (https://viewpoint.pointloma.edu)

To my wife, Ann Cummings. Your inexhaustible love and support not only made this book possible, but you have made my recovery and subsequent ministry a reality. I love you best.

To my kids, Sydney, Ryan, and Joshua Cummings. Your deep grace and acceptance of me during the most difficult times of my life have been the light of Jesus to me. I know Him better because of you.

Contents

Preface

This book isn't anything like the books you've read on stress, anxiety, or depression. Those books are written by therapists and pastoral counselors who have learned from the stories of hundreds or even thousands of sufferers what it looks like to struggle well and overcome significant mental and emotional health challenges, learning to live with stress without letting it break them. Some of those books are amazing, and I have learned more from them than I can recount.

So, what's different about the book that you are holding? Well, for one thing, I'm not a therapist. I haven't spent my career listening to the stories of others and helping them to find health and wholeness in the midst of pain and brokenness. No, in this story I'm not the therapist – I'm the sufferer. In the pages of this book I share with you my own personal journey with stress, anxiety, and depression. To the best of my abilities I try to articulate all that I have been through and the solutions that I have found. This book is personal, *very* personal.

Another difference between *Everybody's Got Bears* and all the other books available on mental and emotional wellness is that I am not only a first-hand sufferer, I am also a trained scientist. I have a PhD in Microbiology and serve as a Professor of Biology at Point Loma Nazarene University. I have taught diverse courses in cell biology, biochemistry, microbiology, infectious diseases, microbial ecology, tropical ecology, and neglected tropical diseases. Beyond the classroom, I direct a research program focused on the genetics of antibiotic resistance among bacteria like *E. coli* and *Salmonella*, bacteria that can kill us if we are unable to treat the infections they cause. You will find that I take a scientific approach to understanding and explaining mental illness in this book, but in a way that anyone can understand.

Finally, the last reason this book is different from all the others you've read (or thought about reading) on the subject of mental and emotional health is that I am a devout follower of Jesus Christ. Sure, many Christians have written books on this subject, some of them very good books. But I have yet to find a book written in the first person, from the perspective of someone who has personally experienced significant anxiety and depression, who is both a biomedical scientist and a person of deep and defining faith. At the end of the day, God is my Father, Creator, Provider, and Lord.

Self-awareness is not my strong suit. Long before I knew I had a mental health problem, I became physically ill. It was like my body was saying, "Alright, if you're not going to listen to your brain, maybe you'll listen to *this*!" I had no other choice but to sit up and take notice of my unhealthy lifestyle and lack of coping and resilience skills.

Let me be clear about something: I am not a therapist. I have no formal psychological or medical training, nor do I have a clinical license or experience, and I don't see patients. I'm also not a pastor or lay counselor in any formal sense. I'm not the doctor – I'm the patient. Like you, I am on a journey. I still struggle with my mental health. I still have setbacks from time to time. But I am learning all I can, and I've been sharing my healing journey with whoever will listen. My problems won't look exactly like yours, and neither will my solutions. What has worked for me may not work for you.

This book is not intended to be a substitute for seeking professional help. I have come to believe that there is nothing more valuable in your pursuit of good mental health than recruiting a set of professional eyes and ears to look and listen in on your situation. Trained therapists and counselors can be objective because they have no skin in the game besides looking out for your best interests. And they've heard and seen it all. You can't surprise a therapist, no matter how crazy your thoughts and behaviors seem to you. You're not the toughest case they've ever known. You won't stump them with your mess, and there is something to be said for sharing your burdens with someone who won't judge or condemn you for your struggles and failures.

My sincerest desire in writing this book is that people like you will find hope and encouragement on their own journey toward a mentally healthy place. Furthermore, I hope and pray that by becoming psychologically healthy, you and I will become more of who we were made by God to be.

Look up the Bible verses I cite, either as a direct quote or by paraphrasing. Read it for yourself, with your own eyes. If you don't own a Bible, there are many online Bibles available for free. Just search the book and chapter you're looking for, and you can read the verse in its original context.

I honestly couldn't be happier for you right now! No, I'm not pleased that you're having a tough time in life. But I am thrilled that you're actually doing something about it. So many people are overwhelmed, depressed, and feeling hopeless, but so few of them are taking any steps to find healing and restoration. You're different. You don't want to stay stuck in the pit. You know how good life can be, how good God intends it to be, and you want to live that life. I congratulate you for being on the journey, not willing to stay stuck in the pit but instead ready to do what it takes to recover the joy, love, and peace that your heart tells you are possible.

As you read this book, you may find it helpful to refer to the other resources I have created just for you at www.davidedwardcummings.com. There you will find video blogs, written blogs by guest writers, links to episodes of the SoulCare Podcast, and an archive of Mental Health Reminders. I send out the Mental Health Reminders weekly to subscribers, so add your name to the list on the Subscribe page if you'd like to receive weekly encouragement. I hope and pray that you are immensely blessed by my story and that you find hope and courage for your own journey.

Dave Cummings
San Diego, CA
April 2019

A BEAR IN MY CAMP

The Natural Role for the Fight-or-Flight Response

"The pleasure of being alive is brought into sharper focus when you
need to pay attention to staying alive."
Richard Louv, *The Nature Principle*[1]

The campsite was beautiful, a dense thicket of gray-black Blue
Oaks, their dark green tops piercing the bright blue Sierra sky. And
the smell – oh, the smell! If you've spent any time in the Sierra
foothills, you know the smell I am talking about. It's the dusty,
pungent smell of decaying oak leaves and sticky bear clover, also
called mountain misery because of how its gooey sap sticks to
everything it touches. I looked around the area, taking in all the
sights and sounds and smells of the forest, deeply breathing in the
unadulterated mountain air.

I'm home.

My motorcycle rested quietly near the fire ring. It had been a
windy, buggy seven-hour ride north that day in September, and I was
tired, sore, and ready to get my feet on the ground. My rear end felt
like I had been on a week-long cattle drive. I found a mid-elevation

campground in the Sierra foothills just outside the entrance to my destination, Sequoia National Park, where I dismounted and set up camp for the night.

It was 1989, and in those days I owned only a 1983 Honda CB550 motorcycle – nothing with four wheels or doors. I had bought this bike when I was in high school, and it went everywhere with me. I learned to ride on the wet and cold streets of the eastern US, so California riding was comparatively easy.

I set up my small camp, parked the motorcycle on the only flat spot at the site so it wouldn't tip over, and laid out a bed about twenty feet from the fire. I had to bring everything I needed in a backpack and a milkcrate bungeed to the passenger seat of my bike, so I didn't have enough space to bring a tent or a sleeping bag. The plan was just to make a bed of soft leaves and branches and sleep under the stars and a Mexican serape I had bought in Tijuana earlier that summer.

I lit a small fire and heated up a can of pork and beans for dinner – classic cattle drive food – then cleaned up the site in preparation for a peaceful night of sleep.

I knew the Sierras were home to thousands of bears, so to get rid of the scent of pork and beans, I held the empty can over the fire and let the flames lick up into the open end to burn off all the syrupy liquid that clung to its ribbed inner lining. It gave off the sweet smell of a summertime barbecue. I dropped the can into the fire to keep de-scenting it while I moved the remainder of my supplies into the large metal bear box provided at each campsite. To my surprise – and delight! – inside the bear box was a fully inflated pool float, the kind you lounge around on with a drink in your hand, drifting in a backyard swimming pool on a hot July day. Someone must have used it as a sleeping pad and left it behind. So I replaced my oak leaves and branches with the mattress and settled in for the night with a contented smile on my face.

It was a beautiful night: dark blue except for the light of the stars and the three-quarters moon that looked down on me from the heavens. I drifted off to sleep with a deep sense of peace along with gratitude and eager anticipation of things to come. I couldn't imagine a more perfect setting.

I awoke with the moon directly overhead – maybe a couple hours after first dozing off. The darkness had deepened from blue to black and despite competition from the dazzlingly bright moon, the stars shone brighter than I had ever remembered.

But something stirred that woke me from my peaceful sleep. Still in a bit of a fog, somewhere between sleeping and waking, I raised just my head to have a look around the campsite. As I did, I saw the back end of a huge, black, furry animal walking away from me, appearing all the larger because of my supine position. A bear!

Startled, I held my breath. My heart was pounding so hard I was sure the clever beast would hear it. I felt my hands shaking under the serape and I was now wide awake – the mental fog was gone. No more musings about the beauty of the stars. I was infused with such a surge of energy I think I could have leapt to the top of a nearby tree in a single motion. Without a sound, I repeatedly mouthed the words, "Holy smokes! Holy smokes!"

It only took me a second to apply my high school geometry skills to the route the bear was taking. It was just a couple of feet beyond my recumbent form, and it was walking in a direct line away from me, perpendicular to my body. I quickly surmised that it had either walked up to me and made an abrupt 90-degree turn toward the fire ring, or it had stepped over my legs, not even noticing that I was there. That image didn't help my panic.

Maybe if I lie still enough it will think I'm a log and ignore me.

The bear first checked out my motorcycle, nudging it with its head. Then it began snorting through the ashes of my fire, a thin line of smoke still rising from the failing embers.

The can of pork and beans!

It brought its head up from the ashes with the empty can on its nose. For another minute or so, the enormous animal fought with the tiny can, trying to get its broad snout in far enough to lick the tasty goo left behind. Then it did something even more terrifying, something I will never forget. Letting the can drop from its nose, the bear quickly shot its head around to look directly at me. We made eye contact.

Uh oh. This is it, Dave. Do or die.

3

As if it hadn't noticed me before, the bear swung around and began trotting towards my still body. I don't know if it thought I was a log full of beetles or maybe some other curiosity – or maybe a carne asada burrito wrapped in a serape tortilla! But whatever it took me for, it wasn't as scared as I was, and it clearly wanted to know more about this strange sight on the forest floor.

Unlike the browns and grizzlies of the northern Rockies and Alaska, the black bears we have in California don't see humans as food. In Yellowstone, for example, a bear trotting towards you is the stuff of real-life campfire stories. Encounters with grizzlies don't often end well. Black bears, however, don't eat people.

But for all I knew, this one was going to begin pawing at me to see if I had any berries or bugs to eat inside me. Sort of like a giant piñata. And I wasn't going to wait to find out if I was right.

I had read enough about bear encounters to know that the best thing to do with a black bear is to look big and intimidating and make a lot of noise. So, in one swift move, when the bear was still about eight or ten feet away from me but closing in fast, I jumped up out of my bed, throwing the serape into the air, my arms raised high, and began yelling.

"Ahhhhhh! Go on! Get outta here!"

The bear, startled at this jumping/screaming log/burrito, put on the brakes and ran in the complete opposite direction. It lumbered across an opening in the trees to the next edge of the forest, turned back to me as if to ask itself, "Did that really just happen?" and disappeared into the woods.

Meanwhile, I stood motionless, arms still high in the air, trying to catch my breath. The silence and isolation were almost as terrifying as the bear. My heart was thumping and I shook all over. *Did that really just happen?* After a short period of time – I'm not really sure how long I stood there – I was able to begin thinking clearly again. My heart rate and breathing were slowing, my palms began to feel less clammy, and I slowly lowered my arms. All the while, I didn't take my eyes off the place in the woods, across the nearby opening, where the bear had disappeared.

Is it over? Is it coming back? What do I do now?

Looking around, the only other people in sight were in a big RV at the other end of the campground. I didn't even know what time it was, but I grabbed a flashlight and walked over to the RV, knocking sheepishly on the door. Funny, but I was feeling a little embarrassed by my response to the incident. No matter – I knew I needed to tell another human being what had just happened.

An older man wearing a worn flannel and jeans answered the door, looking a little puzzled. I told him about my close encounter of the bear kind and he nodded with understanding. "Well, there are bears around here. Have a good night."

As he closed and latched the door to his RV, I realized that I was on my own.

I walked back to my site, lost in thought. The forest didn't seem so peaceful to me anymore. I cursed the deep darkness that had held me captivated in mystery and majesty just a few hours before.

If only it was daytime. If only I had a tent.

That last thought was really silly, but so laughably human. *If only I had a tent.* As if somehow having a thin layer of nylon was going to keep me safe from an angry bear. No, it wouldn't keep me safe, but at least I would be able to ignore anything happening in the forest. Ignorance is bliss, right? If the bear came back and wandered around the camp, I'd just rather not know.

I spent the next several hours sitting up on my pool floaty mattress, shining my Maglite Mini in the direction of every little sound I heard, every snap of a twig, every crackle of a dry oak leaf. I was sure the bear was going to come back with its buddies to teach me a lesson.

There wasn't going to be any sleep tonight.

Since that first frightening encounter, I have had many run-ins with bears of all sizes. I've seen them on the trails up close and through the lens of a camera from a distance. I've watched some of them get into trash dumpsters, and I've witnessed others tear into decaying logs in search of a meal of insects. I am undoubtedly more careful in the wilderness now, knowing that there are bears out there, but I've had to come to terms with it if I want to be able to continue to enjoy the mountains and all they have to offer. Bears can be found just about everywhere in the Sierras, and they are not going anywhere any time soon. I suppose I could give up camping, hiking, and fly fishing, but for me that would be quitting and letting the bears win. Instead, I've learned to take precautions to keep the bears out of my campsite, and I've learned how to chase them back into the woods when they do show up.

Not surprisingly, everyday life is filled with risk and danger as well. Just stepping outside the front door exposes us to the possibility that we will be hurt or even killed.

We face other dangers as well, maybe less obvious, but equally threatening in our minds. Jobs can be lost, cars can break down, relationships can fall apart. With our schedules filled to capacity and no room for anything unexpected, deadlines and pressures at work can make life feel like more than we are prepared to handle.

We are designed to be able to handle incredible stressors in our lives, but only in short doses. My few minutes with the bear in Sequoia wasn't more than my mind and body were ready to contend with. Imagine if it had returned an hour later, and then again an hour after that. Imagine if my irrational fears had come true, and it came back with a few more bears to terrorize me all night.

Now imagine if that pattern repeated itself night after night. It wouldn't take long before my mind and body began to crack under the stress. Yes, we are designed to handle more intense stressors than any of us will likely ever face, but we need to *reset* ourselves between stressors in order to be able to face them. The so-called fight-or-flight response that saved my life in the mountains that night was never meant to protect me day in and day out without time to recover.

WE ARE DESIGNED TO BE ABLE TO HANDLE INCREDIBLE STRESSORS IN OUR LIVES, BUT ONLY IN SHORT DOSES.

Unfortunately, that's often how we live our lives. We push harder and harder each day, trying to get ahead, trying to make life work in this ever-demanding culture. We tell ourselves that if we can get through this week, this month, this year, things will be better. We've been taught that "pushing through" the tough times is the best approach.

But the years go by and we discover that nothing has changed. In fact, if anything, life is even harder, expectations are even greater, and we are still strung out, spread thin, overwhelmed, and exhausted. The result is that our crazy-busy lives can put our nerves on constant high alert, just waiting for the next crisis to show itself. We have more money and more technology than any culture in history, and yet we are more stressed and overwhelmed than ever before.

Without time to reset our minds and hearts, the barrage of stressors takes its toll on our mental, emotional, physical, and spiritual health. It's as if we're living life with a bear on the loose, just around every corner, waiting to pounce.

I wrote this book because I spent about ten years with a bear on the loose in my life. I kept telling myself that things were going to get better, that I just needed to tough it out, to push through.

I'VE GOT BEARS. YOU'VE GOT BEARS. EVERYBODY'S GOT BEARS.

But instead of pushing through, I broke. My physical health crashed, and not long after, so did my mental and emotional health. This book is about my journey from living life with a bear on the loose to chasing the bear back into the woods where it belongs and learning a set of life strategies for keeping the bear out of the camp entirely. My goal is to give you reason to have hope as you face down your own bears. I want you to know that you're not alone and that you that can actually make changes that will make your life better.

I've got bears. You've got bears. Everybody's got bears. But no one has to live life with a bear on the loose.

A BEAR IN MY LIFE

When Fight-or-Flight Invades Everyday Life

"Part of every misery is, so to speak, the misery's shadow or
reflection: the fact that you don't merely suffer but have to keep on
thinking about the fact that you suffer. I not only live each endless
day in grief, but live each day thinking about living each day in
grief."
C.S. Lewis, *A Grief Observed*[1]

My illness started off harmlessly enough. It began with a simple
belly ache during a Sunday morning church service. Pastor Phil was
saying something about the deep stirring of the Holy Spirit when I
felt a deep stirring of a different kind. I excused myself in a hurry
and eventually returned to my seat reciting a list of everything I had
eaten in the past twenty-four hours: Cheerios and decaf coffee before
church, chicken with rice and veggies for dinner the night before,
quesadillas and salsa for yesterday's lunch, and eggs and toast for
breakfast the day before. Nothing stood out as suspicious. We'd just
have to wait and see. No big deal.

Monday – no improvement. Tuesday – a little worse. Wednesday
– body aches and what felt like a fever set in. Thursday – more of the
same. I was supposed to head up to the mountains that weekend –

not far from where Yogi Bear and I first met years ago – for a few days of fly fishing with friends. I was really looking forward to getting on the river, but it wasn't clear if I was going to be able to make it. My initial plan for the fishing weekend was to push through and just deal with it. That always works out well, right?

But about twenty minutes into what was going to be a seven-hour drive, I was miserable. My body was aching, my head was spinning, and my belly felt like a mud pot in Yellowstone, gurgling, slurping, and burping. I told my buddy Ryan I didn't think I was going to be able to do it, and we turned around and headed home. I spent the rest of that day in bed, deeply disappointed and feeling like a failure.

It felt like a combination of an intestinal infection and the flu. Not the so-called "stomach flu," which is really an intense, short-lived gastroenteritis, but actual respiratory influenza. It was lasting too long to be gastroenteritis and influenza doesn't typically cause intestinal problems. It wasn't making any sense.

Sometimes I think I know more about human health than I actually do. I am certified in Wilderness Advanced First Aid. I have a PhD in Microbiology. I teach college courses in microbiology and infectious diseases. I direct a research program on the genetics of drug resistance in bacteria. It seems logical that I should be able to diagnose this illness, right? The problem is that I am not a clinician. I don't see patients – I see students and the inside of a laboratory. I may know a lot *about* pathogenic microbes and infectious diseases, but my day-to-day experiences consist of Petri dishes of bacteria and pages of As, Cs, Ts, and Gs representing their DNA.

Unfortunately, lots of diseases feel like the flu: meningitis, malaria, hantavirus, Ebola, leukemia. My mind was swirling with the possibilities, and I was starting to worry. The more I worried, the more my health declined.

When my symptoms hadn't improved by the end of the first week, I decided I needed to see a doctor. It being a Sunday, my family physician wasn't available, so I checked in at the local urgent care. As I sat waiting in the sterile, white exam room, I studied the diplomas on the wall: a bachelor's degree in Biology, an MD degree, a residency certificate, and a license from the state of California to practice medicine. Those diplomas and certificates gave me confidence in the doctor's credentials.

Before long, the attending physician on duty entered the exam room. She was a woman in her 50s, tall with long blonde hair hastily tied up in the back that made it look like she was in the midst of a very long shift. She immediately struck me as a no-nonsense woman, a trait I appreciate in a doctor.

THE MORE I WORRIED, THE MORE MY HEALTH DECLINED.

"So, what brings you in today?" she asked, taking a seat on a stool next to the exam table where I sat.

I described the signs and symptoms I had been experiencing over the previous week. She took notes on her computer while I spoke, interrupting to ask clarifying questions.

"What time was that?"
"This was on Sunday or Monday?"
"Was there blood in your stool?"
"How is your relationship with your wife and children?"

I appreciated her thoroughness.

She ordered the standard panel of stool tests: inflammatory markers, ova and parasites, and bacteria (*E. coli*, *Salmonella*, *Shigella*, and *Campylobacter*). There's nothing like walking out of the lab with a kit for collecting your own poop, including a conspicuously large catch basin that looks like a plastic sombrero or a serving dish for guacamole dip. But I was more concerned with my health than my dignity, and I desperately wanted a diagnosis so that treatment could begin as soon as possible. So, I dutifully collected my poop, scooping dollops into pre-labeled containers of mystery liquid, homogenizing the suspension like a glass of Ovaltine.

If only this was Ovaltine and not poop soup.

I was convinced that I had giardiasis. *Giardia* is a single-celled parasite covered in multiple whip-like tails called flagella. Even though it is just a single cell, *Giardia* is larger and more complex than bacteria. It lives in the feces of cattle and other animals, including some wildlife, without causing them any harm. They poop it out, and the rain and snowmelt relocate it to the nearest water supply, either underground or at the surface. Giardiasis is often thought of as a backpacker's illness because people in the backcountry sometimes fail to purify the water they collect from streams and lakes and end up infected. The symptoms I was experiencing were a good match for *Giardia* infection, all the way down to the texture and smell of my stool (I know, gross, right?).

There was one problem: I hadn't been camping or backpacking yet that year. So where could I have picked it up? My best guess was that I got it from an employee at a restaurant - maybe my favorite taco shop – who had giardiasis. But within a week the lab tests all came back normal. No sign of parasitic worm eggs, infectious bacteria, inflammation of the intestinal tract, or *Giardia*, which would have been seen in the ova and parasites test. Nope. All normal.

That can't be right. Do the tests again.

The clinic obliged and we ran all the tests again, along with a couple more. All normal.

What? No way. I'm still sick. There has to be a pathogen. One more time.

All normal for the third time.

How could that be? How could I be so sick, and yet no infectious agent could be detected?

It didn't make sense.

I steadily got worse after that, confined to bed for much of the morning, venturing only as far as the living room couch in the afternoons. For some reason, the mornings were much worse for me. I awoke to abdominal pains, fever-like aches, and vertigo. Sometimes the room spun so much I had to swing a leg out of bed and onto the floor to try to ground myself. Honestly, it felt like a horrible hangover.

My muscles were buzzing with tension, like an electrical current was running through my legs and back. I squirmed and clenched my muscles, trying to make the electricity stop. Sometime around midday, the symptoms would retreat enough that I could try to shower and relocate myself to the family room. By evening, my spirits were up, most of the symptoms, except for the extreme fatigue, were bearable again, and I could allow myself to feel hopeful. But I dreaded going to bed, knowing that the cycle would start all over again in the early morning hours.

Soon I lost my appetite, nauseous but unable to vomit and losing weight every week. My body ached, though I could never detect a fever. I grew weaker, both from lack of nutrition and from the illness itself. I could usually make it from the bed to the bathroom, but anything further might require a shoulder to lean on. When I bathed, Ann would help me into a plastic lawn chair she had set up in the shower. My dignity was deteriorating along with my health.

At this point, I was still sick – worse than when it started – and we were no closer to answers than when we began. I was getting nervous. I took a couple weeks of vacation time, but classes at the University were going to begin soon and I was in no shape to prepare, much less teach, my classes.

What if I am still sick? What if I am worse instead of better? What if I am never able to return?

The doctors should be able to figure this out. *I* should be able to figure this out.

I finally decided to contact my department chair and warn her of my situation. Unlike in elementary school, I am the only person on our campus that can teach my classes, and the students who registered all needed these classes to advance towards graduation. The University was going to have to hire a couple of adjunct professors for the semester to cover for me. I was going to have to take a medical leave of absence.

Much to my relief, I was told to focus on my health – my job would be waiting for me in January.

Honestly, that was the first good news I had received in weeks. One of my greatest worries up to this point had been my job. There is very little else I know how to do well besides teach science and do research. If the University felt it had to cut me loose, it wasn't clear to me how we would pay the bills. Like most Americans, we probably only had a couple of months' cash in reserve for such an emergency. That wouldn't buy me enough time to find another college to hire me, so the University's assurance that they had no plans of letting me go any time soon brought the first deep sigh of relief I had felt since this ordeal had begun.

Thank you, God.

Soon, though, the details of my situation crowded back into my mind: declining health, normal test results, no diagnosis, and now a medical leave of absence from my job – the worry inside me was growing to near panic.

What if this is permanent and I'm going to be disabled and incapable of ever returning to work? Who will support my family? What if my illness is fatal? My three kids don't deserve to grow up without a father. I still have so much I want to do with them and teach them.

I was catastrophizing, playing out the scenario to its most gruesome possible end.

During the first month, my primary care doctor and the urgent care doctors were not especially concerned, nor did they see my situation as particularly urgent. I felt like no one heard me, or if they did, they didn't really care. I could think of nothing else, every hour, every day. For me, there was nothing more urgent than finding some answers and some relief. So I insisted on seeing a specialist, starting with a gastroenterologist. My worst symptoms were in my belly, so this seemed like the best place to start. After a consultation, we decided that it was most likely dietary, so I began testing different foods by cutting them out one at a time: dairy, wheat, gluten, fructose, to name a few. Every so often I'd think we figured it out ("I'm lactose-intolerant – hooray!") only to find that the pattern wasn't consistent.

And so began a month-long series of visits to other specialty departments. Cardiology – healthy heart. Neurology – healthy brain. Oncology – no sign of tumors or blood diseases. Otolaryngology, endocrinology, infectious diseases – healthy, healthy, healthy. Always healthy. Two different doctors commented that I was the healthiest sick man they had ever seen. That didn't help. How could I be "textbook," "a picture of good health," or "going to live to be

100"? I was so weak I could barely get to each of these appointments, so how could I be the poster child of a healthy colon or a fit heart? It just wasn't adding up, and my head was getting too muddled to process it all clearly.

AT SOME POINT WHEN YOU ARE SUFFERING YOU JUST WANT ANSWERS, ANYTHING OTHER THAN, "YOU'RE PERFECTLY HEALTHY."

All of these normal test results had mixed effects on my emotional state. On the one hand, I was relieved to know I had no sign of a brain tumor, Crohn's disease, or Meniere's disease. I also did not have any parasites or other microbes trying to make a meal out of me. Endocrinology assured me that there was nothing inherently wrong with my adrenal glands or other hormone-producing organs. On the other hand, I wasn't getting any better, but was, in fact, growing more ill with each passing week. At some point when you are suffering you just want answers, anything other than, "you're perfectly healthy." I knew I wasn't perfectly healthy, and soon, no news was just bad news.

Fast-forward a month and a half. The room was dark. Even though it was mid-day, the shades were drawn and I was in bed. To my left sat my wife, Ann, coaxing me to sip through a straw from a bottle of Ensure. To my right, my father-in-law, John, was holding my hand – although it was more like I was clinging desperately to his – while Vickie, Ann's mother, prayed aloud.

The scene was something straight from the movies. Ann took on an in-charge tone of voice, the kind a nurse takes with her patient in the hospital. "Come on now, Dave. You know you need some nutrition in you to fight this. Take another drink now."

My 14-year old daughter, Sydney, sat by her mom's side with an expression of calm control, as if nothing was wrong that wouldn't be made right soon enough. Josh and Ryan, both younger than their sister, peeked into the room from the hallway, whispering to one another.

I hated the thought of not being able to be the one caring for my family. Instead, I was the cause of their fear and uncertainty. They were worried about me, caring for me. That was *my* role, not theirs. I was supposed to be the one worrying about *them*, caring for *them*. All at once I felt both helpless and guilty.

What if it's cancer? What if I have to face chemotherapy and radiation? Do I have the strength to do this? What if it's terminal? Who will provide for Ann and the kids? They'll lose the house, for sure. Ann will have to go back to work, but to do what? She dropped out of college to put me through graduate school. *If she can't find good work, will the life insurance policy be enough to get them by?*

I had been sick for several weeks at that point, and I wasn't getting any better. In fact, at that point I was confined to bed much of the day because of weakness and dizziness.

John and Vickie exchanged fearful glances that spoke volumes. They were old enough to have walked alongside their parents through significant illnesses and even death. Having raised six children, they were no strangers to scary times. Just ten years before my illness, they said goodbye to their youngest son, Sam, after an eighteen-month battle with leukemia. If you've held a loved one's hand through terminal illness, then you're familiar with the ups and downs, the good days and the bad days.

Seeing me in such a state must have brought back old memories, old fears, feelings of helplessness in John and Vickie. After all, my health had been steadily deteriorating without a diagnosis.

Could we be facing yet another life-threatening illness? Could life really deal our family such a bad hand to lose two of us just years apart from one another?

One afternoon, the distress and discomfort had become so severe, and I had grown so distraught, that Ann took me to the ER. I didn't know what they could do for me, but I hoped that my presence there

15

would lend some urgency to the issue. Until that day, I had been stuck in the system, visiting one doctor, referred to another, and waiting from one to four weeks to see the next specialist. No one seemed to be in much of a hurry but me. Every hour was miserable and getting worse. I needed to get their attention, and the ER seemed the best way to do this.

Surprisingly, it was in the ER where I found some much-needed comic relief. I was checked into a bed next to an elderly woman who had apparently fallen and broken her hip. Either she didn't remember falling or she was afraid of being put in a home, because she denied anything had happened. "I just decided to lie down in a sunny spot on the floor when those EMTs burst in the room."

She was feeling little pain except when the nurses would move her. Then she would scream and make threats like a woman in labor who had opted out of the epidural. Only seconds after they would stop moving her, she would settle down again and begin talking about how nothing had happened at her house, least of all a fall that broke her hip. Eavesdropping on that conversation made me smile more than I had in many weeks (does that make me a bad person?). But there was still this matter of an undiagnosed illness.

The young doctor on duty pulled away my curtain and looked at me gravely. He had been reading my chart and my electronic record and was very concerned that no diagnosis had yet been reached. I appreciated his scientific, problem-solving approach to my condition. He didn't reduce me to a case, sending me away with a standard medication. Nor did he dismiss my frustration and fears. Instead, he treated me like a friend in need. We could use more doctors like that.

Besides a good laugh at the expense of the woman next door to me, two more good things came from that ER visit. The first was when the doctor ordered an MRI scan of my brain for that very hour. He wanted to rule out a tumor. This had already been ordered, but was not considered urgent and was thus scheduled for another week away. He also moved up a CT scan of my abdomen to look for abnormalities. I had to drink what seemed like gallons of barium sulfate – a tart, metallic liquid that provides contrast with the soft tissues of the gut. The worst part, though, was the nurse coming in every few minutes to tell me I had to drink it up faster. Of course, by the time I was strapped into the CT machine I had to pee like nobody's business, but wasn't allowed to move. More normal results. More relief and frustration.

The doctors, it seemed, were running out of ideas. And I was running out of hope. Something had to change.

PLAYING DOCTOR

The Dangers of Self-Diagnosis

"Do not be wise in your own eyes; fear the Lord and shun evil.
This will bring health to your body and nourishment to your bones."
Proverbs 3:7-8

On any given day, dozens of people call me "doctor." I am
Doctor Cummings to my students at the University. I am introduced
as Doctor Cummings when I speak at a conference or event. I even
tried to get my kids to call me Doctor Dad, but they weren't buying
it.

I remember clearly the first time anyone called me "doctor." It
was November of 2000, and I had just defended my dissertation
before a committee of scientists with PhD degrees in biology,
microbiology, soil science, and geochemistry. The north Idaho sun
had already set and the temperature was dropping fast. I shivered
outside the century-old brick building on the University of Idaho
campus, pacing up and down the sidewalk while the committee
deliberated inside (where it was warm, of course). After making me
suffer for a few minutes, my graduate advisor, Frank, a tall southern
man with a bushy mustache that always seemed to drip with his last

sip of coffee, came out of the building with a smile on his face and his hand extended to me.

"Congratulations, *Doctor* Cummings," he said as he shook my hand, emphasizing the word "doctor" with a proud smile.

I had passed my defense and was welcomed into this elite club of people who stayed in college far too long trying to avoid getting a job.

Most Americans associate the title "doctor" with a medical doctor. And sometimes it's assumed that I'm a medical doctor too. After all, I talk about and work with infectious diseases every day. No matter what others might think, though, I'm not *that* kind of doctor.

I have tremendous respect for medical doctors. Their training requires four years of college (usually in a really tough major like biochemistry), another four years of medical school, two to six years of residency, and often a multi-year fellowship, all before they are working independently. In medical school, student doctors usually begin seeing patients under the supervision of a senior physician beginning the third year of medical school. By the time he or she is seeing patients independently, a doctor has treated thousands of people under the tutelage of mentor physicians. The 30-hour shifts, the sleepless days and nights, the relentless stress, the pressure of knowing that lives are in their hands each and every day: I feel a little guilty taking the title "doctor" knowing that others have had to sacrifice so much more to achieve the same title. It would be like giving a Boy Scout the title "Navy Seal." I'm just a Boy Scout.

NO MATTER WHAT OTHERS MIGHT THINK, I'M NOT *THAT* KIND OF DOCTOR.

Sometimes, though, I forget that. Sometimes I hear the title "doctor" so often that I begin to believe that I actually have the clinical skills to diagnose an illness or prescribe an appropriate therapy. Usually the patients are my kids a friend. You can see how tempting it would be for me to diagnose myself. I was suffering from symptoms common to many microbial infections, those caused by bacteria, viruses, or parasitic worms. And I know a few things about these life forms. I am a doctor of microbiology, right? I know a few things about these life forms. So, in my own health crises I decided that I was going to diagnose myself.

I'm sure the *real* doctors just loved me. I was that guy who thought he knew more than they did. I requested specific lab tests and if the results were negative, which they often were, I insisted that they be run again. For every new visit to a specialist I proposed a new answer to the riddle of my sickness. But time and time again I was wrong. Test after test showed that my body was healthy. One overworked endocrinology resident snarked that I'd had the "million-dollar diarrhea workup."

Really? Listen buddy, I'm sure you haven't slept in the last 24 hours, but I haven't been able to walk unassisted for nearly two months. So just back off!

Eventually, we just want answers, even if the news is bad (can I get an amen?). The lack of any diagnosis, or even a hint pointing in a particular direction, was vexing as I got progressively weaker and sicker with each doctor visit. Between a lack of appetite and the loss of everything I ate before sufficient digestion, I lost weight rapidly. I'm not a big man to begin with – 5'10" and about 170 pounds in those days, but I had quickly withered to a mere 150 pounds, my old high school weight from 25 years before. I needed a change of strategy.

Cue the Internet.

The Internet has arguably been the most transformative invention of the 20th century, maybe even of all human history. Never before has information flowed so freely and so rapidly around the world. It has changed our independence by providing the average person with step-by-step instructions for things once only performed by skilled professionals. YouTube videos cover just about any do-it-yourself job you can think of from replacing the alternator on your 2001 Ford Ranger to converting that old oak TV cabinet into an armoire for your teenage daughter.

But all this information - and misinformation - at the fingertips of virtually every human being on the planet doesn't come without its dangers. Anyone with an Internet connection can post anything they like to the Web without being held accountable for accuracy. Misinformation, opinions, and outright lies are just as welcome as facts. The discernment skills necessary to safely navigate the content of the Internet today are far beyond what was required in the days when our sources of information had been first vetted by people with presumed expertise. The world of information and ideas has changed effectively overnight.

You see where I'm going with this. One of the many dangerous allurements the World Wide Web provides is the temptation to diagnose our own illnesses. We mistakenly believe that (1) most information on the Internet is reliable, and (2) armed with good information, we can do as good a job as a doctor at diagnosing illnesses and prescribing a remedy. Neither of these, however, is a safe bet.

The next time you have a cold, Google your symptoms. In ten minutes, you'll be convinced it's not a cold but rather lupus. Search for causes of that twitch your eye does every night before bed and soon you're telling your mother on the phone that you have Parkinson's disease. The next time you are vomiting, don't be surprised when the Internet informs you that you only have a few months to live due to a brain tumor. While there is indeed very good information on the Internet, the reader often has to wade through swamps of misinformation and unqualified opinions to find the good stuff. And it's often difficult to recognize the good stuff from the garbage. Without the savvy to tease out who the sources of information are, how they have gathered and assessed the data, and what their motives are for convincing you one way or the other, interpreting information on the Web can be nearly impossible sometimes. To think that I could do just as good a job of diagnosing my illness with the right information as a doctor, with all of her years of training and experience, is like thinking I could build an Audi S8 because I picked up the Chilton Guide!

No, if the Internet has taught us anything, it has taught us that information alone is not enough. Safe and accurate diagnosis requires wisdom that only comes with experience working with patients in a clinic, making self-diagnosis a very risky business. The knowledge and understanding that come from decades of training and treating a couple thousand actual patients cannot be replaced by twenty minutes on the Net, no matter how clever one is.

You would think that as a trained scientist I would know better, but I was growing desperate, so I turned to the Internet for answers. I felt like the white-collar heroin addict sneaking around the seedy part of town in the dead of night, hoping no one would recognize me. Giardiasis, Ebola hemorrhagic fever, Addison's disease, multiple sclerosis, brain tumor. My head spun with the possibilities, and my fear swelled to a crescendo. One after the other, however, the doctors ruled out the most serious alternatives, leading to relief mingled with fear and frustration.

When I first fell ill, I wasn't particularly concerned. An upset stomach for a few days could be anything. But as the weeks passed without improvement or answers, I began to worry. I began asking fearful questions, "what if" questions. And my frantic Internet searches and self-diagnosing were only making things worse. My health was worse than ever, and I was nearing panic.

IF THE INTERNET HAS TAUGHT US ANYTHING, IT HAS TAUGHT US THAT INFORMATION ALONE IS NOT ENOUGH.

Apparently, the Internet is full of bad advice – who knew? Unfortunately, so are many of our well-meaning friends and family. Steeped in good intentions, they share with us what they heard on talk radio or read online. They tell us what worked for them, the assumption being that the same thing will, or might, work for us as well. What some people fail to realize, though, is that your mess is just as special as you are. You are unique, your mess is unique, and your solutions will be unique too.

During my illness, when the doctors were stumped and I was becoming increasingly ill, I received much well-intentioned advice and even diagnoses from friends and family. Everyone had met someone with the same symptoms as mine who had a vitamin deficiency or an allergy or who had been exposed to lead in the water supply. I never faulted anyone for trying to help – it was clearly out of love that they wanted to help fix me. I understand that it feels good to help. It feels so much more productive than just listening or checking in with the struggler every day. It feels good to be needed and to be helpful. But as my friend Mike pointed out to me, sometimes it's easier to try to fix someone than to empathize with them and walk through the struggle by their side. That was what I really needed.

Rather than help, though, the barrage of advice I received during my crash just overwhelmed me even more. It's true that hurting people sometimes need to be pointed in the right direction. But once they are under the care of professional, trained doctors and counselors, the best thing we can do for them is to pray, listen, and be available. Throwing in our own amateur two cents may simply make matters worse.

Desperate times call for desperate measures. As a scientist, I am normally a skeptic of alternative medicine, not because I don't think there are some approaches that work for some people in some situations, but because there is a lack of repeatable scientific evidence to back it up. Conventional, modern medicine may have its flaws, but at least there is a tremendous amount of data behind it. In science, every decision we make is based on evidence, and this attitude carries over into the rest of my life. But I had become desperate enough to consider anything that might provide either answers or relief. We looked into acupuncture, yoga, massage therapy, meditation, herbal remedies – anything that someone somewhere claimed would help. I reluctantly scheduled an appointment at a naturopathy clinic after a phone consultation in which the woman at the other end promised results. We were about to change strategies, but in a direction I wasn't particularly comfortable going.

Before embarking down the naturo-path, however, I was examined again (all too thoroughly!) by the gastroenterologist. Since the worst of my symptoms were in the gut, and because every other specialist had declared me normal and healthy, I was putting all my hopes in this visit. It sounds strange to say it, but I was actually *hoping* he would find something. I was miserably sick, but no one had any answers. I was ready for a diagnosis.

I was dreading this visit. I knew what the follow-up appointment entailed. I had heard all sorts of stories about probes boldly going

where no man had gone before. When the nurse called my name –
"Mr. Cummings?" – my mind raced with ways to get out of it. I
could just sit there and pretend I was Mr. Smith. I could run for the
door and head to the car before they had ahold of me. Maybe I could
fake a heart attack and they'd have to send me downstairs to the ER.
I gave Ann a pitiful look, pleading with my eyes – *If thou be willing,
remove this cup from me*. With a casual wave of her hand she shooed
me along to follow the nurse and returned to her book.

After some time, I awoke out of a daze, not having been
completely unconscious but floating around someplace between
aware and unaware. The doctor stood over me.

"David, how do you feel?" he asked in a thick African accent.

He had just completed two procedures that will drain away any
remaining dignity in a man. The first was an endoscopy – inserting a
camera outfitted with a sampling tool through the upper digestive
tract from the mouth, through the esophagus, and into the upper
reaches of the small intestine. The second was a flexible
sigmoidoscopy – similar to the endoscopy but going in through the
out-door, exploring the lower two feet of the colon. At this point I
might have preferred a diagnosis of cancer over yet another round of
normal results. "Textbook," he called me. My digestive tract could
not have looked any healthier. It seemed impossible.

*Something is clearly wrong with me - and growing worse - but no
one seems to know what.*

I was at the end of my rope.

Almost as an afterthought, he added an observation that has since
changed my life.

"You know," he said, leaning in close, "I have seen these same
symptoms in people suffering from chronic stress."

THE *REAL* DOCTORS

Accurate Diagnosis and the Slow Road to Recovery

"None of us, doctor, parent, or friend, can truly enter into another person's pain. It is the loneliest, most private sensation."
Paul Brand, *The Gift of Pain*[1]

My boys like to wrestle with each other. Most brothers do. It usually starts with one of them throwing a casual elbow at the other while passing in the hallway as an invitation for battle. If the invitation is accepted, there might be some minor tussling to begin with, each boy feeling out the other. Smiles are big despite the grunts of effort to knock the other one over. Once they hit the floor, the real contest begins. Arms are wrapped around heads, legs are wrapped around torsos, grunts and groans emanate from the scrum. A couple minutes in, it becomes apparent to onlookers (my wife and me) that the intensity has picked up a bit. One boy slugs the other, and it is returned with a little more force than the original. Neither boy wants to be one-upped by his brother, so more force is used with each volley until all smiles and laughter are gone and sniffles and snorts of anger can be heard from the cloud of dust. By the time we separate them, one or both is usually crying and blaming the other for some unfair blow.

Illness and anxiety can behave like a couple young brothers, feeding off one another and gradually amplifying one another's symptoms. Illness or pain can often lead to anxiety.

What's wrong with me? How long will this last? What if I don't fully recover?

You may find it surprising to know that anxiety can cause physical symptoms of illness (more on this later). Regardless of which comes first, the anxiety or the illness, the two can cycle between one another, spiraling downward until it seems impossible to break free from the grip of either.

I had worked myself into a frenzied state, and now it seemed like my mind was deteriorating as quickly as my body. The worse my symptoms became and the longer we went without answers, the more I worried and envisioned catastrophic consequences for my family and myself. The experts call this "health anxiety," when we worry so much about our health that it becomes a diagnosable mental illness by itself. The real trouble with health anxiety, at least in this situation, is that it can feed a vicious cycle by exacerbating your physical health problems.

I was caught in a downward spiral. As my physical health deteriorated, my anxiety increased, leading to a further worsening of my physical health, and so on. And the real bugger was that I couldn't see it. I was in too deep to see what was happening to me.

We began retreating from functions like attending birthday parties and church services. Family vacation was put on hold, as were all of my much-anticipated house projects. Ann had just begun working for the church. But she had to step down to stay home and care for me full time. I had to tell the University that I was not going to be able to teach my fall courses, which were going to start in about two weeks. What had started out as a minor tummy ache had completely altered our lives.

Even so, when the gastroenterologist suggested that chronic stress could mimic the symptoms of a number of bodily illnesses, I was incredulous and a little offended.

Chronic stress? Are you kidding me?

26

It felt like he was saying, "It's all in your head, buddy – just get over it." Besides, it was summer, the most relaxed my schedule ever got.

To understand where I was mentally and emotionally at the time, you have to understand the life of a college professor at a liberal arts university. Nine months out of the year, my schedule is intense. From September through May, I teach classes in cell biology, biochemistry, and microbiology. Most courses meet one hour per day, three days a week. Then each of my classes also have a required lab as well, claiming another three-hour chunk of time, once a week. All told, I typically spend fifteen to twenty hours per week in the classroom or the laboratory directly teaching my students.

Then there's all the preparation and grading. Each hour of lecture requires several hours of preparation, and each lab period requires many more hours in advance to ensure the best possible hands-on learning experience for the students. As an undergraduate college, we have no grad students to teach our classes or labs for us. This is a great benefit to the students, but comes at a high price to the professors.

Work often follows college professors home, at least the ones I know. So, in addition to a forty-hour week on campus, we often bring grading and other work home with us on evenings and weekends.

And then there's the seemingly endless procession of various administrative duties. There are committees to serve on, university functions to attend, accreditation to assess and support, and programs to continuously review.

The bottom line is that the life of a college professor isn't too different from the life of a college student: late nights, long hours, little personal time, and a relentless pace. The difference is that we are expected to keep this up for thirty to forty years rather than the typical four to five years that a student attends college.

I find it rather amusing that some people have publicly speculated that being a college professor must be a very low-stress career.[2] That certainly has not been my experience. The largest survey of college professors across the US reports that a third of all faculty have considered leaving academia altogether in the past two years because of the stressful conditions.[3]

27

As busy as the school year is, in the summer I can work a straightforward forty-hour week and bring nothing home with me. My evenings and weekends are free to spend with my wife and kids or work on a project around the house. It's like a vacation.

I direct a research program in microbiology where we spend our summers studying bacteria and their DNA as scientists rather than students. In the summer, I feel like an artist who has been away from his craft for too long. The work is energizing and exciting. It refreshes me between school years by reminding me of my passion for the practice of science.

Such was the setting when the well-meaning gastroenterologist suggested that maybe my illness was not physical in nature, but psychological.

Chronic stress? Are you serious?

I wasn't convinced. Ann and I went home that afternoon, discouraged and afraid. I could think of a million reasons why chronic stress was not an accurate diagnosis. The problem, of course, was that this left us right where we had started. Two months of declining health and no clear explanation, which meant no clear path forward to recovery.

ILLNESS AND ANXIETY ARE LIKE A COUPLE YOUNG BROTHERS, FEEDING OFF ONE ANOTHER AND GRADUALLY AMPLIFYING ONE ANOTHER'S SYMPTOMS.

It seemed that I had two options: either visit the naturopath to see what she thought of my condition, or make an appointment with the Psychiatry Department in my health care system. I wasn't particularly excited about either road. I was uncomfortable with the first because of its reliance on testimonial evidence rather than scientific rigor; the second just seemed plain wrong to me.

After much prayer, I called Psychiatry and made an appointment for an initial assessment.

One endlessly long week later, I was sitting next to Ann in a therapist's office, waiting to be evaluated. The room was somewhat sterile, with a couch along one wall and a professional office chair on the other. A desk sat between them. On the wall were generic photos of beaches and an ocean. It could have been any beach, any ocean, anywhere. Something about the room, though, gave me a sense of peace and calmness, despite its clinical asepsis. If the source of my illness was psychological, someone here would be able to identify it. I was confident that I was in good hands.

Before long, a middle-aged woman with dark, shoulder-length hair and a professional suit stepped into the room and shook our hands with a smile. She introduced herself as Aednat (pronounced ey-nit), and by her accent I guessed that she was Irish or Scottish. Indeed, she told us, she was born and raised near Dublin and came to the US for graduate school in clinical therapy. Her role, she explained, was to perform initial triage on new psychiatric patients. She would evaluate me and help decide my next steps.

I told Aednat about the past two months, of how I had fallen ill and progressively worsened. I told her of all the specialists we had seen, and the repeated refrain of "healthy and normal." I shared with her about the visit to the gastroenterologist who had suggested chronic stress. Then I went on to make my case for why I thought this couldn't possibly be the source of all my troubles. I gave her my rehearsed pitch like a lawyer's closing arguments. I was sure I had won my case and would be acquitted of all charges of psychological disorders. Surely, this educated woman, this experienced therapist, would see that my illness had its roots in something biological, something other than the brain.

But Aednat was not so easily convinced. "So, the past couple of months have been restful – that's great. Tell me about the past several years."

Hmm. I hadn't thought about that.

I honestly hadn't taken the time to evaluate the past decade when considering my illness. Evidently, reflection is not one of my strengths.

So, I rewound ten years to our transition from Idaho back to California. During that time period we faced loss and grief, major changes, and a heavier workload than ever before. When I got around to telling Aednat about the death of my step-brother, Jason, I found it hard to find my voice. Until that point, I had stayed objective in recounting our ups and downs, but when she asked how

I had grieved Jason's death, all I could think to say was, "There wasn't any time."

I suddenly realized that that one sentence captured my life for the past ten years: *There wasn't any time.*

There wasn't any time to grieve Jason's death, or the death of my good friend Mike, or the death of my youngest brother-in-law, Sam. There wasn't any time to fix up my fixer-upper house or work in the yard on weekends. There wasn't any time to throw a baseball with my young children, or to build a fort with them in the yard, or to wrestle with them on the living room floor. There wasn't any time to reflect on the happenings of life. Instead, the pace of life demanded that I move on immediately. So, that's what I did, obediently marching forward - always forward.

Aednat scribbled something on her notepad.

"David, you've been through a lot recently," she said looking up. "But your life has gotten so busy that you can't even take the time to process it all."

I knew she was right.

"I think you're suffering from generalized anxiety disorder, and possibly depression as well," she continued. "I want you to see a therapist and a psychiatrist to discuss the possibility of medications. Are you comfortable with that?"

I was more comfortable at that moment than I had been in months. It was like a forty-pound backpack had been lifted from me after two months on the Appalachian Trail. We knew our next steps. All I could do was weep.

We had a diagnosis, finally!

I had just spent the past two months physically sick and in pain, too weak to get out of bed, and my mind reeling in anguish, thinking about what could be wrong and how this story was going to end. When the therapist confidently diagnosed me with generalized anxiety disorder with a side of depression, I wept from the overwhelming sense of relief. I was so ready to fix this problem.

Just prescribe the pills for me Doc and I'll be on my way.

Ah, but it's never that easy, is it?

With infections caused by viruses, we often don't have any medication to provide a cure or even relief. We have to trust that our immune systems can handle it, and they usually do. In contrast to viral infections, one of the things I love about bacterial infections (does that sound strange?) is that they typically respond to antibiotics very quickly. In most cases, your child's ear infection or your urinary tract infection can be taken care of with a little pill in just a few days. Some medications can even be formulated to taste like strawberry milk! Unless you are infected with one of the antibiotic-resistant superbugs, most of the time, antibiotics represent a quick fix.

But there's a darker side to this quick fix, and that's how it affects our expectations. Nowadays, we expect to be able to repair all illnesses and injuries in a jiffy with no long-term side effects or consequences. Break an arm skateboarding? A cast for six weeks, or worst-case scenario a three-hour surgery, and you'll be back at the skate park in no time. Clogged arteries from a lifetime of greasy food and a sedentary lifestyle? No problem – we've got a pill for that. When my youngest son Josh was 10 years old, he said something to me that was really profound.

"Dad," he said from his seat next to me in the car, "I bet people wouldn't drive so crazy or take so many chances if we didn't have good doctors."

Mercy! The wisdom of a child!

Although we can often fix a broken bone or clear clogged arteries in short order, there really are no quick fixes when it comes to our mental health. As I slowly discovered in the coming days and weeks and months, it had taken me a lifetime to dig this pit I was in, and climbing out again was not going to happen overnight.

After my diagnosis in Psychiatry, I thought for sure I'd be escorted double-time to a psychiatrist who could get me on the right meds and then into therapy where we'd figure out what went wrong in my brain and how to turn it around. And we did, but not double-time. The first appointment offered to me was two weeks out. There was nothing available before then, the receptionist apologetically told me. I was having a hard time imagining another day of this misery, much less two more weeks. They put me on a wait list and said they'd call if someone cancelled before my appointment.

THERE REALLY ARE NO QUICK FIXES WHEN IT COMES TO OUR MENTAL HEALTH.

Unfortunately, this was how it was before my diagnosis, and nothing seemed to change after it. There was no sense of urgency in anyone other than me and my family. It was as if no one understood my pain. And they probably didn't. Dr. Paul Brand, quoted at the beginning of this chapter, reminds us that no other person can experience what we are experiencing inside.[1] The best we can do is describe it to them and hope they can relate, even just a little. I did receive a good deal of empathy from the people I came into contact with in my health care system, but there was little they could do to speed up the process. I was beginning to see that just navigating the complexities of an overwhelmed health care system was going to slow my recovery to a frustrating pace.

But a slow health care system was least of my obstacles to recovery. I soon learned that even if the system could have sped up things at their end, the mind heals slowly. The brain is a fascinating organ made up of trillions of specialized cells called neurons, as well as other cell types. We used to think that nervous tissue like the brain was a relatively rigid material, such that once it formed a pathway, that route was firmly fixed for life. We've since discovered that the brain and its neurons can grow and change and heal, but it happens very slowly. This concept is called neuroplasticity.

In our early development, the brain is growing new neurons, forming new connections, and changing almost daily. The neonate starts life on this earth with an average of 2,500 neural connections (called synapses) per neuron. That means each nerve cell is talking to another 2,500 nerve cells. By the time a child is three years old, that number jumps to over 15,000 synapses per neuron. New input, for better or for worse, during these early years takes shape as neurological pathways in the brain. The young mind is something of a blank slate.

By the time we are adults, though, we have dramatically slowed the formation of new neurons and synapses, and our brains have even begun to prune away some synapses that are not getting much use. Our average neuron now only forms about 7,000 synapses, and these have been carefully selected to be of the most use to us. All further changes are done slowly and carefully, maximizing energy and resources. It is no wonder, then, that the unhealthy psychological pathways we have spent years building are not going to be reconfigured overnight.

THERE IS EVERY REASON FOR YOU TO BELIEVE THAT YOU CAN FIND HELP FOR YOUR OWN STRUGGLES.

The months and years following my diagnosis have been defined by an intentional commitment to building resilience in the face of stressors: reading books, attending classes, seeing therapists, sharing my story with others and listening to and learning from their stories of how they have been terrorized by their own bears. Never again do I want to invite a bear back into my camp, and when one shows up uninvited I want to be ready to chase it back into the woods.

In later chapters, we will explore the many coping strategies I have learned over the years that have contributed to my growing stress-resilience. You should come to peace now, however, with the fact that there are no quick-fixes, no easy solutions, no one-size-fits-all answers. Even so, there is every reason for you to believe that you can find help for your own struggles, that you are not the toughest case ever known to man, unredeemable, destined to suffer. It's undoubtedly going to take hard work and might require an entire lifetime to accomplish, but if you are ready to live life bear-free, let's get started!

NOT ALONE

The Epidemic of Stress, Anxiety, and Depression

"What has been will be again, what has been done will be done
again; there is nothing new under the sun."
Ecclesiastes 1:9

In the fictional novel *The Martian*, astronaut Mark Watney is left
behind on Mars as the rest of his crew barely escapes in the midst of
a horrible storm.[1] Assuming he was dead, they take off just in time
to save themselves from an ugly death-by-sandblasting. Watney
spends the next year and a half alone on Mars, desperately trying to
survive each day. While he has superhuman problem-solving skills
as an engineer and a botanist, his greatest challenge, what consumes
his thoughts every day is establishing communication with Earth.
Without this lifeline, he knows that he will eventually die, no matter
how clever he is.

Sometimes in life we can feel like we've been abandoned to die
on a deserted planet. Either by choice or by circumstances, we find
ourselves all alone, struggling to survive each day. No matter how
smart we are, no matter how clever or ingenious we are, nothing is
going to get better unless we make contact with the outside world.
Once Mark Watney established communication with planet Earth, he

was no longer alone in his fight to survive, even though he felt a million miles away (or to be more precise, 33.9 million miles away!). In fact, without his knowledge, most of the people on Earth had been watching him, cheering him on, praying for him. They couldn't bring him back – he had to do that on his own with the help of NASA and other experts – but his entire outlook changed once he realized that he was not alone. He was less afraid, he had more courage to face the long journey ahead of him. The unknown was less scary, and he knew he could pull through.

I BEGAN TO BELIEVE THAT I COULD LEARN AND GROW THROUGH THIS EXPERIENCE, THAT I COULD RECOVER AND BUILD RESILIENCE TO FUTURE EPISODES OF STRESS, ANXIETY, AND DEPRESSION.

I felt like Mark Watney, lying on my bed, all alone. No one could possibly understand what I was going through. No one could help me find my way back to a healthy, safe place again. I wondered if I was going to die here, alone, on my own Mars. But as people reached out to me, as I learned that, unlike Mark Watney, I wasn't the only person in this predicament – as I learned that others had experienced similar struggles and emerged victorious, I began to believe that I could also learn and grow through this experience, that I could recover and build resilience to future episodes of stress, anxiety, and depression.

Not alone

When I was first diagnosed with generalized anxiety disorder and depression, I was embarrassed, maybe even a little ashamed. I felt like I should be able to handle the stressors of my life. After all, it seemed like everyone around me was handling their crazy lives just fine – so why not me? But I've always had the attitude that I want people to accept me as I am, warts and all, so I took a deep breath and summoned the courage to push back against the sense of shame and embarrassment and I told people what was going on. Instead of condemnation or silence, people responded with their own stories of panic attacks and irrational fears. They told me about their ten-year battle with depression or their dread of leaving the house. It became clear to me very quickly that I was not alone in my fight, and soon the shame and embarrassment faded into the background as I began sharing my story more publicly, first on the social media stage, then on literal stages at my college and in my home church and at other churches that would have me.

The response was always the same: thank you for giving us permission to talk openly about our struggles!

It turned out I wasn't alone after all.

Mental Health Statistics on Adults in the United States[2]

>50%	Will be diagnosed with a mental health disorder at some point in life
31.1%	Will experience an anxiety disorder someday
20%	Experience a mental health disorder in a given year
18.1%	Live with an ongoing anxiety disorder
16%	Have been too depressed to go to work at least once this past year
14%	Have been too anxious to go to work at least once this past year
6.9%	Live with ongoing major depression
44,965	Committed suicide in 2016

Data from reliable sources like the Centers for Disease Control and Prevention and the National Institutes of Health reveal just how prevalent mental illness is in American culture. If you're in a crowded room right now, take a minute to look around you. One in five of the people you see are struggling with either anxiety or depression, and some of them are unlucky enough to have both. Sooner or later, a third of them will experience clinical levels of anxiety, and at least half of them will eventually be diagnosed with one mental health disorder or another. One or more of them may feel so hopeless as to be contemplating suicide, even right now. Still think you're alone in this?

In the Christian church

"But Dave," you might protest, "I'm sitting in a group of people right now who are all Christians. Surely, they aren't struggling in the same ways as the rest of the world. They have Jesus!"

While I do believe that Christ is the ultimate answer to what ails us, I haven't seen anything that makes me think that these numbers are much different inside than outside the church.

There aren't many quantitative studies available that focus specifically on mental health among the churchgoing population. Anecdotally, I can tell you that I have met countless people in my own church (weekly attendance of about one thousand) who are struggling in the very same ways as the general population. For example, the first time I offered a weekly class on anxiety and depression, more than fifty people walked through the door on the first day. I offered a workshop on anxiety and depression at a church of about six hundred in a small town in Oregon and nearly two hundred people showed up. This doesn't happen if mental health struggles are minimal in the church.

Some writers have made the claim that mental illness is just as common in the church as in the rest of society, but more studies need to be done to support this argument. In her book *Troubled Minds*, Amy Simpson cites a survey she did in 2010 of readers of Christianity Today publications asking about their experiences with mental health in the church.[3] Almost a quarter of them (23%) reported that they had personally experienced an anxiety disorder. This number is close to the lifetime anxiety rate (31.1%) and the ongoing anxiety rate (18.1%) of the general population,[4] suggesting that the claim that just as many people in the church suffer from mental health challenges as the rest of the US population may have some merit.

It may come as a surprise to you to know that your pastor is human, too! Protestant pastors in the US reported struggling in many of the same ways as the general population in the course of their ministries: depression (46%), marital problems (26%), parenting problems (27%), and addiction (19%, mostly pornography).[5] Nearly a quarter of our pastors confess that they have seriously doubted their faith at some point, and more than a third are at medium to high risk of burnout in their jobs right now.[6] Most pastors rate their mental and emotional health as "excellent" (32%) or "good" (36%), but almost half of them (46%) have dealt with significant depression.[6] Pastors are more likely to feel inadequate about their work (57%) than other adults (30%), and more likely to feel mentally and emotionally exhausted (75%) than people who are not pastors (55%).[6] Are mental health problems a part of church life? You better believe they are!

Our youth

Kids today may have more on their plates than any previous generation. Single parents, gender confusion, moral relativism, legalized recreational drugs, and troubling current events all conspire to make it difficult for our youth to discern right from wrong, good from bad, truth from lies. Is it any wonder they struggle? This uncertainty compounds the natural turmoil of adolescence, leading kids to respond with violence, rebellion, and rejection of their parents' values. School shootings are on the rise across the country. Every year more kids who grew up in the church are leaving in search of their own spirituality.

According to findings from LifeWay Research, 66% of young adults who previously attended church or youth group dropped out of church for at least a year after high school.[7] Of those, only 31% returned within a short period of time.

As adults, we have a tendency to get a bit nostalgic about our high school and college years. We selectively remember all the good times, the friendships, and the excitement of gaining our freedom. We remember our first crush, our first date, our first kiss as if it were all from a series on the Hallmark Channel, complete with sappy romantic music and soft lighting. The further away from our own high school and college experiences, the more warmly we remember the good times and the less we can recall the struggles. We selectively forget the incredible inner turmoil of being an adolescent and the pressures from all around us to be whatever it is everyone else expects us to be: an all-star athlete, a 4.0-scholar, a world-class pianist, a mature Christian, one of the popular kids. We forget about the sexual identity crisis nearly everyone experiences during and just after puberty. We block out the feelings of not fitting in and the overwhelming need to be accepted. When the classic rock station plays "Don't Stop Believin'", your mind doesn't go back to the late nights studying for that Biology exam or the pressure to get a good SAT score. No, you remember Saturdays at the beach and video game competitions among friends.

Mental Health Statistics on Youth in the United States[2]

75%	of all lifetime cases of mental illness begin by age 24.
50%	of all lifetime cases of mental illness begin by age 14.
49.5%	will experience one mental disorder or another before age 19.
31.9%	of teens experienced an anxiety disorder in 2016.
12.8%	of teens had one or more major depressive episodes in 2016.
11%	will experience a mood disorder (mostly depression) during their teens.
8%	will experience an anxiety disorder during their teens.
7.5%	of 6- to 17-year-olds used psychiatric medications for emotional or behavioral difficulties in the past 6 months.

For many of us, our memories of high school were that it was some of the *best years* of our lives, so we naturally tell our kids to expect the same thing.

"You are just going to love playing high school sports."
"Senior prom is just a magical time for a young woman. You're going to be so beautiful."
"Enjoy these years, because it just doesn't get any better than this."

But the reality is that our kids are struggling and they need our guidance and stable presence more than our reminiscences about our own youthful experiences. For many of them, high school is the *toughest years* of their young lives as they struggle to emerge from their cocoons, unsure of who they will be when they do. My fourteen-year old usually only offers a grunt when I ask how his day was at school. I can brush him off as just being an adolescent pill, or I can dig deeper. Our kids desperately need us to dig deeper, even if they don't want us to.

Listen to these statistics on the state of our youth in the US:

Before we tell our kids that "you've got it easy" or "these are the best years of your life," maybe we should check in with them to find out how *they* feel about life right now. The answers they give may surprise us.

On the college campus

If we felt like we were gaining some freedom in high school, college felt like we were completely independent. Many of us lived away from home for the first time, away from rules and expectations and lectures about getting our priorities straight. No one told us when to wake up or when to go to bed. We could eat whatever we wanted to eat without anyone telling us that we needed more veggies on our plate. I see young men in our college cafeteria eating Lucky Charms for lunch and finishing it off with a few chocolate chip cookies. No one is there to tell them no, so they can push boundaries and finally do whatever they think is best for themselves.

In college, often for the very first time, they can begin to imagine themselves in a career: they can see themselves as a nurse or a journalist. They can begin to see the path towards becoming a doctor or owning their own business. The thrill and excitement brought on by all the possibilities takes their breath away. The world is their oyster, and nothing can stop them from achieving their dreams.

DESPITE BEING SURROUNDED BY THOUSANDS OF OTHER YOUNG PEOPLE IN THE SAME LIFE STAGE OF DEVELOPMENT, LONELINESS ABOUNDS IN COLLEGE.

If you went to college, then chances are that you have similarly rose-colored memories of those years. You fondly think back to the late-night study sessions with friends and the comradery of pushing through the hardest classes. You go back to the burrito runs and the movie nights and the double dates. Nostalgia tells you that college was all deep friendships and bonfires at the beach. Again, your mind dwells on all that was good and wonderful and better-than-now from your college years, and you want those same things for your own kids.

No, you don't hang onto the memories of how much you clashed with your parents or fought with your siblings. You don't cling to thoughts of all the pressure in college to keep up good grades and maintain scholarships and get into graduate school or land that first job. You've forgotten about all the pressure to find a "soulmate" in college and begin that next phase of your life. Instead, your mind takes you back to the good memories, and slowly but surely, the tough times fade into the gray until eventually you actually believe that life was in fact so much better then.

I can tell you from experience, we're not helping our kids by placing so much pressure on them to have the time of their lives in high school and college. Unmet expectations are some of the most powerful drivers of disappointment, which itself can become a key component of anxiety and depression. Truth be told, high school and college are not always all they are cracked up to be. Many students find these years to be filled with deep struggles and self-doubt. The workload can be overwhelming, and the pressure to get good grades has driven more than one overachiever/pleaser/perfectionist to the therapist's office. Despite being surrounded by thousands of other young people in the same life stage of development, loneliness abounds in college.

In my interviews with college students for this book, I have heard stories of immobilizing panic attacks, hopeless depression, deep spiritual confusion and doubt, and an overwhelming sense that no one could possibly understand because everyone else has this college thing figured out. Everyone else, they believe, is having the best time of their lives. They've told me that the major sources of their anxiety and depression include

- Too much to do and not enough time to do it all
- The incessant pace of college

- Worries over grades and getting into graduate or professional schools
- Worries about what's next – job, marriage, life
- Financial worries
- Friend relationship and dating relationship stresses
- Conflict and problems back home.

The National Institute of Mental Health reports that the young adult years (ages 18-25) encompass the highest rates of depression in the United States (10.9%) and nearly the highest rates of all mental illnesses combined (22.1%), second only to 13- to 18-year-olds (49.5%).[8] Our kids don't need us to set them up for major disappointment with expectations of what college life will be like for them. They don't need helicopter parents who try to fix every problem for their college student or who send a letter to the President of the University when a professor treats them unfairly. They don't need parents to demand perfection from them or insist on a particular major and career track. At the same time, they don't need hands-off parents who think that age eighteen means their job as parents is done. And they don't need parents contradicting what they are being taught in college, unless Mom or Dad is actually a trained expert in that discipline.

Mental Health Statistics on College Students in the United States and Canada[9]

80%	report feeling overwhelmed at any given time.
70%	felt lonely in the past year.
30%	felt lonely in the past two weeks.
50%	have been so anxious at some time in college that their grades suffered.
33%	have been so depressed at some time in college that it was difficult to function.
25%	have a diagnosable mental health disorder.

What they do need is stability at home, grace and patience from Mom and Dad as they sort through this new stage of life with all of its trappings and responsibilities, age-appropriate boundaries, and permission to fail. They also need support and coaching to learn how to get back up again, dust off their britches, and get back into the game when they do fail. Above all else, they need assurance that no matter what happens, they are loved unconditionally.

The post-high school years, whether or not they include college, can be incredibly difficult for everyone in the family. Deep patience, unconditional love, and absolute acceptance are what our kids need to support them through the tough times and uncertainties of life, as they fully become all that God has made them to be.

Stigma and silence

Maybe the greatest barrier to overcoming mental and emotional problems is the stigma associated with them, whether that stigma is actual or just assumed. Stigma is the negative judgment that some people make about others based on biases, misunderstanding, ignorance, assumptions, bigotry, racism, or any other skewed way of understanding the individual in question, themselves, or the world. Stigmatized people often feel that they are somehow contaminated, and no one wants to come near them for fear of contaminating themselves.

Stigma doesn't stop with just negative thoughts – those negative ideas, no matter how off-base they may be, can interfere with a person's ability to live a normal life by denying them access to the social, cultural, and economic benefits of society.

When it happens within the walls of the church, the spiritual impact of stigma on the lives of already-hurting people can be devastating. Stigmatized individuals are hindered from taking full advantage of the many resources of the church like fellowship, small group Bible studies, or Sunday school classes. Their personal and spiritual growth can be severely inhibited. They may feel judged or unwelcome, and they may even stop attending altogether.

Stigma is a mark of disgrace placed on someone who is told, directly or indirectly, that they are inferior, unworthy of full participation in life because of their choices or circumstances. It's a product of the world's way of thinking, one in which the weak, the deviant, and the flawed are not welcome. It has no legitimate place in a Christian worldview. It has, however, undoubtedly crept into church culture from the greater culture of the society we live in.

In Paul's letter to the church at Rome he reminded us, "There is, therefore, now no condemnation for those who are in Christ Jesus" (Romans 8:1). If God no longer condemns us for our failures and brokenness, what right do we have to continue to judge and condemn one another, or, for that matter, ourselves?

MAYBE THE GREATEST BARRIER TO OVERCOMING MENTAL AND EMOTIONAL PROBLEMS IS THE STIGMA ASSOCIATED WITH THEM.

Stigma is the result of worldly heart attitudes such as pride, arrogance, superiority, self-reliance, and even fear. Consider what might lead you or another person to be judgmental about the following people who could walk through the doors of your church:

- A single mother checking in her three unruly children to your Sunday school classes
- A member of Alcoholics Anonymous looking for a support group
- A young man addicted to pornography seeking biblical counseling services
- A man recently released from prison for armed robbery who just wants a fresh start
- A homeless woman carrying bags of her belongings
- A young man nervously talking to himself

While stigma has no biblical foundation, it has certainly snuck its way into the church and can be a significant barrier to many. In a 2014 LifeWay Research study, both sufferers (59%) and their families (65%) said that they want to be able to speak more openly at their churches about mental illness, but their pastors are rarely bringing it up, if ever.[10] They inadvertently feel like they are at fault, as if their problems are due to a failure of spiritual devotion or character. All of this silence leads to an increased sense of shame and serves to reinforce the silence. Ed Stetzer of LifeWay Research says that "we immediately assume there is something else, some deeper spiritual struggle causing mental and emotional strain."

So much of church life is social: Sunday morning services, weekly Bible study groups, special events, classes, programs, and virtually everything else we do. But when someone senses that they are not welcome or that they are being blamed for their problems, their reaction is often to isolate themselves from others in the church and pull back from much of community life. They may even stop attending altogether, missing out on vital relationships needed for their recovery and healing.

THE ONLY TRUE ANTIDOTE TO STIGMA IS COMPASSION.

Considering the ways in which stigma presents itself – gossip, exclusion from social events, "should" statements, well-meaning but misplaced advice – you might think that the solution to ridding our churches and our culture of mental health stigma would be to teach people to simply keep their mouths shut. After all, most of our mothers did say to us, "If you can't say anything nice, don't say anything at all." And, indeed, many of us (myself included) could learn to think a few seconds longer before opening our mouths. But since stigma comes out as more than simply words, this approach doesn't change what's going on in the hearts of people.

A more common strategy for combating stigma is through education. The thinking is that we wouldn't be so judgmental about the life decisions and circumstances of others if we only understood what they were going through. If we understood how difficult life is for a single mom, we wouldn't judge her so harshly. If we could walk a mile in the shoes of the porn addict we wouldn't be so quick to condemn him. So we educate people about domestic violence. We teach them about the difficulties of substance abuse and other addictions. We teach children not to pick on the kids who can't afford expensive shoes or who don't read as well as everyone else in the class.

While taming the tongue and learning about the struggles of others are both very important steps in personal growth, and should lessen the impacts of stigma in the church, neither of them gets at the underlying heart attitudes that lead us to shun and shame people who are struggling with their mental and emotional health.

I have come to believe that the only true antidote to stigma is compassion, the ability to understand and share the feelings of someone else. Only then will the judgment we unintentionally impose on others come to an end. Colossians 3:12 says that we are to *clothe ourselves with compassion,* and Romans 12:15 urges us to *have genuine concern for the suffering of others.* This is God's intent for us.

Even when we find it impossible to put ourselves in someone else's shoes, even when we believe that they are entirely to blame for their struggle, a compassionate person withholds judgment and assumes that the person's experience and their response to it are both fully legitimate.

Take a moment to consider how compassion might change the way you respond to the single mom with out-of-control kids, the alcoholic, or the porn addict. How might compassion change the way you see someone with bipolar disorder who isn't able to get out of bed some days? What about the person having panic attacks that can't commit to attending your Bible study? Compassion – a heart attitude deeply rooted in Scripture – dissolves away stigma, opening up opportunities for fellowship, growth, healing, and recovery.

A common response to experiencing stigma is to go silent, to hide underground and hope our problems just go away. If we keep our problems to ourselves, we rationalize, no one will ever have to know or have reason to exclude us. Silence, however, merely serves to keep us far from the things we need the most, like friends, family, and God.

As damaging as silence is, it appears to be the norm in the modern church. Most (98%) of leaders surveyed by Amy Simpson[3] confessed that they were aware of people with mental health disorders in their congregations, yet only 13% felt that mental health and illness were discussed in healthy ways in their churches. Something isn't right here.

It's crucial that we understand that the silence surrounding mental health struggles in the church goes both ways: sufferers are not speaking up about their problems for fear of stigma and isolation, and the rest of the congregation is afraid to reach out to these people for fear of being drawn into their drama or for simply not knowing what to say or do. If I see a young man sitting in the back row with his head in his hands in obvious anguish, do I sit down next to him and ask if he's OK, or do I hope that someone else knows him well enough to help? When a woman in the lobby tells me that she and her husband are getting a divorce, do I tell her I'll be praying for her and shuffle out as fast as I can, or do I take the time to listen to her story?

Compassion isn't easy. It requires us to take risks and be vulnerable, neither of which is particularly comfortable. Wise King Solomon repeatedly implored his readers to openly, humbly seek advice.

- "For lack of guidance a nation falls, but victory is won through many advisers." Proverbs 11:14
- "The way of fools seems right to them, but the wise listen to advice." Proverbs 12:15
- "Plans fail for lack of counsel, but with many advisers they succeed." Proverbs 15:22

In the New Testament, the apostle Paul doesn't beat around the bush either:

- "Therefore I will boast all the more gladly about my weaknesses… for when I am weak, then I am strong." 2 Corinthians 12:9-10
- "Carry each other's burdens, and in this way you will fulfill the law of Christ." Galatians 6:2
- "Be completely humble and gentle; be patient, bearing with one another in love." Ephesians 4:2

Mental and emotional health problems can be tremendous obstacles to experiencing a full life in Christ. At the same time, stigma and silence in society and the church are barriers to the sufferer finding hope and healing. If we desire to help people live an abundant life in Christ, we need to strive to become people of compassion and vulnerability. Through personal and corporate growth in these areas, we have the opportunity to tear down the barriers holding so many people back, and give them the freedom and courage to pursue God with their whole heart, soul, mind, and strength.

SOBER JUDGMENT

The Importance of Honest Personal Reflection

"Made a searching and fearless moral inventory of ourselves."
Alcoholics Anonymous, Step Four

Looking back is not my strong suit. Every time we've moved I have forgotten our previous address and phone number within a couple of months. Rather than making me nostalgic, looking at old photos often surprises me. *Did I wear glasses then? I don't remember that shirt. Who are these other people in the picture? When did we visit that town?* Sometimes it makes me feel more like an outside observer looking in on someone else's past rather than my own.

I am a planner by nature. I love planning trips, events, activities, next steps. I can pore over maps for hours, thinking about all the possibilities. One of my favorite parts of teaching, in fact, is creating the course syllabus each new semester. I get excited laying out what we will do and learn for the next few months. There is no doubt that I love to look forward. This is very likely the reason that I struggle more with anxiety – fear of what *could* happen – than depression, which is often fueled by disappointment and regrets for what *has already* happened. My constant looking forward and rarely ever looking back kept me on the run, never healing from old hurts, never processing my emotions, just plowing forward into the great unknown.

Therapy revealed to me that I had been living my life with a bear on the loose for the past ten years. I had grown so tense that I was continually on high alert, waiting for the next emergency, the next urgent request on my time, expecting the worst just around every corner. There was a bear waiting for me on campus when I arrived in the morning, and it was roaming the hallways when I got home again at the end of the day. It even showed up at church on Sundays when I just wanted to experience a Sabbath rest with the Lord in fellowship and worship. It seemed like there was nowhere I was free of the fear that a bear might jump out at me at any moment. I was exhausted and ashamed that I couldn't handle it all. How did I get here in the first place? How did I let things spin so out of control that I couldn't get through the day without being on the edge of panic at any moment? That was the million-dollar question that I had to face if I was going to recover and begin rebuilding resilience into my life.

In my first visit with the psychiatry department, Aednat called me out for not considering the past decade of my life and all of its stressors. With one simple question, she made me aware of the fact that I had not been adequately reflecting on and intentionally processing my struggles: "So, the past couple of months have been restful – that's great. Tell me about the past several years."

I had simply pressed on with life's demands immediately in front of me, never looking back, never asking "what just happened?" Apparently, that's not a good thing.

I've since learned that honest personal reflection is essential to wellness. We need to acknowledge what we have done and what has been done to us, and ask ourselves how we feel about these things. I was in a rush to get the pains of the past behind me and move forward to the hopeful future, but our wounds will not heal if we do not attend to them. If you are emotionally challenged like me, you may want to ask yourself some very specific questions such as,

- What just happened?
- In what ways am I responsible for this?
- How does this make me feel?
- Should I be angry about this?
- Do I need to grieve this loss?
- What can I learn from this experience?

It's understandable why many of us avoid this kind of personal reflection: it is usually not a fun process. In fact, it can be painful and upsetting. It can shake our self-confidence and make us feel weak or broken, both of which we actually are in some ways. But without this self-awareness, we leave ourselves vulnerable to much more intense and complex struggles further down the road. Unresolved, or unaddressed, challenging life events hurt our relationships, our work, our ministry, and our effectiveness in life.

HONEST PERSONAL REFLECTION IS ESSENTIAL TO WELLNESS.

Being thoughtful and reflective about every single decision that comes our way in this complicated, busy world would be overwhelming and leave us incapacitated, so we often switch to autopilot when the stakes seem low and we feel like we can trust our "gut." Dealing with how we have been hurt and the challenges life has dealt us is not the time for autopilot.

Honest self-examination shatters our intentional illusion that all is well. It may require you to scrape off that bumper sticker from your car with the little palm trees that says "No Bad Days", and make you think twice about telling everyone that "it's all good" when they ask how you are doing. Real life includes many bad days. For that matter, it's not always all good. And that's OK.

Sincere, candid self-evaluation is a biblical principle rooted in Scripture. The apostle Paul says to "think of yourself with sober judgment" (Romans 12:3). "Sober judgment" implies the kind of open, honest, brutally truthful reflection that most of us avoid but all of us need. We need to assess our strengths and weaknesses, our successes and failures, the quality of our relationships, our expectations and disappointments. It is critical to our wellness that we consider what we have done and what has been done to us. We need to understand where we have failed others and ourselves. The purpose of this exercise is not to tear ourselves down or to stir up some false humility, but rather to arm ourselves with the truth so that we can make informed decisions that are in the best interests of ourselves and those we love.

Thinking of ourselves with sober judgment means accurately assigning responsibility for hurts. No one, no matter how awful, can *make* you think, say, or do anything. "You made me do it" is a major cop-out. "I wouldn't have said those things to you if you hadn't pushed me" puts the blame for your own words or actions on someone else.

Even our feelings are ultimately our own responsibility. While our initial reaction to someone else's words or actions might be feelings of anger, pain, or sadness, as thinking human beings we always have the opportunity to process those feelings and take action to resolve them. If my wife, Ann, makes an off-hand comment that hurts me, I can blame her for the pain and hold onto it, or I can work through it by telling her how it made me feel and ultimately forgiving her for it, whether she admits any wrongdoing or not. If I continue to blame her for how I am feeling, I am going to stay stuck there and eventually hurt the relationship more than the initial offense ever could have.

In their best-selling book *Boundaries*, Drs. Henry Cloud and John Townsend say, "your feelings are *your* responsibility and you must own them and see them as your problem so you can begin to find an answer to whatever issue they are pointing to."[1] This means that while someone else might be the cause of my initial feelings, it is on me if I remain stuck feeling that way.

As human beings, we sin against God and other people. The word "sin" is so unpopular and ugly. It's much easier to use euphemisms than to own our sin. We'd rather say we "made a mistake" or "screwed up" than to say that we sinned, but that's just sugar-coating our true nature. Scripture says that all of us have sinned and fall short of God's righteous standards (Romans 3:23). The Bible calls "sin" everything we say and think and do that is contrary to God's teachings. Personal reflection, honest, deep, true self-analysis, requires that we call our sin exactly what it is: sin.

Your drinking problem cannot be pinned on your abusive and alcoholic father. Your pornography problem is not your cold and uninterested wife's fault. Your angry outbursts at your co-workers are not because you are Italian and everyone knows Italians have bad tempers. Making excuses for your own sins may make you feel better about your choices, but it does nothing to heal your wounds and love the people around you. Excuses do nothing to advance your walk with the Lord.

SOME OF US BEAR THE WEIGHT OF RESPONSIBILITY FOR THE CHOICES OF OTHER PEOPLE, BRINGING FEELINGS OF GUILT, SHAME, AND UNWORTHINESS THAT ARE NOT OURS TO BEGIN WITH.

Similarly, you and I are not responsible for the words and actions of other people, even when their words and actions are in direct response to our own. We cannot control the thoughts, feelings, or actions of others, but we can control our own actions, and to some degree our own thoughts. We can't control the way someone else speaks or acts, but we certainly can control the way we respond to them.

It is a sad curiosity that as human beings we are inclined to take responsibility for the hurts caused by other people in our lives. You may have done and said some hurtful things, but you did not force your husband to leave you. You may have been naïve and too trusting, but you are not to blame for being swindled out of your hard-earned money. Couples choose to divorce for a variety of reasons, but no matter what they may say, the children are never responsible for that choice. A child is never at fault for being abused, no matter how difficult or disobedient that child may have been. No victim, adult or child, of sexual abuse is ever to blame for what someone else did to them, under any circumstances. Some of us bear the weight of responsibility for the choices of other people, bringing feelings of guilt, shame, and unworthiness that are not ours to begin with. As often as we take responsibility for the choices of others, we must lay it back down again, refusing to own what is not ours to own.

We need to get better at assigning responsibility where it actually belongs. This is not about blame in the sense of holding grudges or stirring up anger, but instead it is about objectively placing responsibility on the people who are responsible, whether ourselves or someone else. When we make it about blame, one person is the victim and the other is the perpetrator. Labels can leave us stuck, without a clear path forward for healing and reconciliation. Sober judgment is about having all the facts so that we can make clear, sensible choices about how to heal and move on.

In the early part of the 20th century, the American theologian Reinhold Niebuhr is said to have written and published a prayer of desperation and surrender that has changed the lives of countless people since. The opening lines of what is now called The Serenity Prayer (see Appendix C) are familiar to many of us, especially those who have been involved in a 12-step program of some kind like Alcoholics Anonymous or Celebrate Recovery.

"God, grant me the serenity to accept the things I cannot change, the courage to change the things I can, and wisdom to know the difference."[2]

The two principles in these opening lines of The Serenity Prayer will resurface throughout the remainder of this book: accepting the things we cannot change and changing the things we can. The thoughts, feelings, words, and actions of other people fall into the first category, things we cannot change. Our own behavior is in the second category.

Whether we know it or not, we all keep two lists. One contains the circumstances in our lives that are beyond our control or influence. We'll call that first one the Cannot-Change List. The second list, the Can-Change List, is populated with circumstances that we can change, or at least influence. There are some obvious things that must necessarily go onto one list or the other: the death of a spouse and things that have happened to us in the past both belong on the Cannot-Change List, while the choice to quit your job and the words that come out of your mouth clearly belong on the Can-Change List.

For many of us, our Cannot-Change List is far too long and filled with many points that actually belong on the Can-Change List. The problem is, at least in part, wisely called out in Niebuhr's prayer: placing problems on the Can-Change List requires courage. Once we admit to ourselves that we can change or at least influence a struggle in our life, then we're responsible for it. We can no longer blame life for dealing us a bad hand or fate for treating us so poorly. We can no longer blame others for putting us in this miserable situation. Once a struggle in our life has been moved from the Cannot-Change List to the Can-Change List, we're no longer the victim but a participant, even the primary responsible party, in our current unhappiness.

Embracing the role of the victim can be very tempting. When we're the victim, we don't have to change anything. If my weight problem is due to crummy genetics, I don't need to exercise or count calories because it's on my Cannot-Change List. If my multiple failed relationships are caused by the abuse I faced at the hands of a trusted adult when I was a child, there's no point in seeing a marriage counselor or trying to choose to trust again – it's just who I am and that's the way it goes. While some of life's most challenging trials and circumstances may indeed be caused by forces out of your control, taking on the identity of a victim leaves you powerless and stuck right where you are. No one's life changes for the better by staying stuck in the victim role.

As I began the long, slow process of reflecting on my past, especially the incredible stressors and struggles of the past decade, I came to the conclusion that there were many items on my Cannot-

Change List that actually belonged on my Can-Change List. Remember, to qualify something for the Can-Change List I only needed to be able to influence the situation in some way or another, even if I couldn't completely change all of it. The more I applied Paul's principle of sober judgment to my life, the shorter my Cannot-Change List became and the more my Can-Change List grew. That was a little scary.

As Niebuhr reminds us, that Can-Change List is going to require courage to face. Change is never easy, especially when it comes to re-tooling our own situation and mindset. I had believed that there was nothing I could do about the high pressure and stressful nature of my career as a college professor. All of my training was in microbiology, so clearly it was the only way I could support my family, right? Well, not exactly. Yes, I put a lot of years into training as a scientist, but did that mean that teaching a heavy load at a Christian college and trying to direct a research program with undergraduate students was really the only thing I could do to pay the bills? No, it didn't. There are a variety of careers available to scientists, not to mention careers completely outside of science I might have qualified for. Sober judgement required that I move my job from the Cannot-Change List to the Can-Change List. Did that mean I should or would even want to change careers? Not necessarily. Nonetheless, it belonged on the appropriate list so that I could soberly, honestly weigh all of my options for making changes in my life.

NO ONE'S LIFE CHANGES FOR THE BETTER BY STAYING STUCK IN THE VICTIM ROLE.

I didn't change careers – I love the work I do and the people I get to work with too much to walk away from it all. So, I began looking carefully at all of the stressors of my job, putting each one on the appropriate list. In the end, I discovered that much of my stress was actually self-imposed and based on unrealistic self-expectations. And because those self-imposed self-expectations are clearly on the Can-Change List, I made some changes. For example, I learned a new phrase: good enough. That's a difficult thing to say for an overachiever, but for the sake of my personal well-being I had to let go of perfectionism and embrace grace and mercy for myself. I bet you could benefit from a little self-grace too. Am I right?

Accurately assigning things to one list or the others takes time and practice. Let's start with a couple softballs. Assign each of these to one list or the other:

- What you are having for dinner tonight
- What you had for dinner last night
- The person you married
- The person you are going to marry
- The shirt you are wearing
- The shirt your husband is wearing

Got the idea? OK, let's try some tougher examples. Think through each of these scenarios and sort them into the Cannot-Change and Can-Change Lists:

- Your divorce from two years ago
- Your loneliness
- Your job that you hate but pays the bills
- Your noisy next-door neighbors
- Your fear of abandonment
- Your credit card debt
- The abuse you faced as a child
- The abuse you are facing today
- Your recurrent depression
- Your anger problem
- The hurtful things your mother used to say to you
- The hurtful things your mother says to you today
- Your perfectionism
- Your wife's perfectionism
- Your daughter's choice of a boyfriend to date
- Your son's choice of a college to attend
- Your unemployment
- Choices made by the current President of the United States

- What happened to you while deployed overseas
- Your PTSD, panic disorder, major depression, schizophrenia, bipolar disorder, or any other
- psychological disorder you are facing
- Unanswered prayers
- God's love for you

Learning how to properly sort life's curveballs into either of the two lists is an important skill for recovering from and building resilience against stress, anxiety, and depression.

Working through my two lists was one of the first and most important steps in my recovery from anxiety and depression. All of a sudden, I was in the driver's seat again, seeing with new eyes where I could make changes to my life without wholesale starting over again. Remember, to qualify for the Can-Change List, you only need to be able to influence the situation, even if you can't, or shouldn't, outright change everything. You can start to see now that the Can-Change List is the power list. It's where life's struggles and trials begin their journey towards improvement and healing. But it takes honesty and courage to put anything on that list in the first place.

Interestingly, moving items in the other direction, from the Can-Change List to the Cannot-Change List, is equally important and also takes a certain degree of courage, especially if we have been fighting to change something or someone that is beyond our influence. The two most obvious types of hurts that do not belong on your Can-Change List are (1) things that happened in the past and (2) other people. I cannot reach back in time and change my parents' divorce any more than I can prevent the dinosaurs from going extinct. As obvious as that sounds, many of us keep past hurts on the Can-Change List, not necessarily *believing* that we can change history, but simply *wishing* that things had gone differently. While wishing that the past could have been different isn't in and of itself harmful to our well-being, dwelling on what should have or could have been, keeps us from moving forward and healing. It prevents us from living today and making the most of the good things in our lives right now.

Similarly, the hearts, minds, and behaviors of other human beings are beyond my capacity to exert change. Each of us is an independent entity, responsible for our own choices. Believing, or even just hoping, that we can change another human being inevitably leads to pain and disappointment.

God, grant me the serenity to accept the things I cannot change...

"Serenity" is one of those words that has lost much of its original meaning in today's culture. It is most often associated with tranquil nature scenes, like a beautiful sunset with a bird flying through stately trees, or maybe a deer in a flowery meadow. The Latin root, *serenitas*, referred to calm and clear skies or seas. When used to describe a state of mind, serenity implies calmness, peacefulness, a lack of turbulence. Do you see Niebuhr's goal in choosing this word to describe his desired state-of-heart for facing his Cannot-Change List? He's asking God to bestow on him a sort of divine resignation as he learns to accept the people, past, and circumstances that are beyond his ability to change. Only with a heart like calm seas and clear skies can we lay aside our futile, frustrating attempts to change these things and trust that God can and will work them out for the good of His kingdom (Romans 8:28), even if they do not work out in our own personal short-term interests or according to our personal plans.

This is, at least partially, what the Bible means when we are encouraged to lay our struggles at the feet of Jesus (Psalm 55:22, Matthew 11:28-30, 1 Peter 5:7). The serenity to accept the things we cannot change, divine resignation in the face of people and situations that are out of our hands, laying our burdens at the cross – these are all word-pictures for prayerfully releasing control over to the Lord. Though we often pick up those burdens again, we can still turn to God and give them right back.

We will never be free to face our Can-Change List until we can stop carrying burdens that were never meant to be ours.

...courage to change the things I can...

While the Can-Change List is indeed the power list, it takes courage to put items on it in the first place, and even more courage to take action. For example, once I accepted that I could actually change my situation by changing jobs, I had to decide if it was worth it. Every choice comes with trade-offs; there are very few decisions that do not have some consequences we must contend with. If the demands of my career were literally killing me, I could change the situation. I always had the right to leave my job at the university, to walk away and start over again doing something different. No one was holding me there against my will.

But I would pay a heavy price if I went that route. For one thing, I love the work I do. I'm passionate about microbiology (just take my word for it), I love the people I work with and our Christian mission, and there is nothing more satisfying than pouring myself into training and mentoring young people. Then there's the paycheck, which is kind of necessary if we want to keep our house and stuff. And let's not forget how difficult it can be to move - changing jobs, friends, churches, schools. Walking away from my job would come at a very high price.

Once I began to analyze my work situation more deeply, I realized that while it might not make sense to change careers, there were numerous changes I could make. Alterations to my attitude, my perfectionism, and even my workload could make a tremendous difference in the stress I was experiencing. To start, I learned a new phrase: "good enough." That wasn't part of my vocabulary until my unrealistically high self-standards almost ruined me. I began to set limits on how many hours I could work on a particular activity and how much work I was willing to bring home with me.

Another new word I had heard but hadn't used myself was "no." I discovered that I didn't actually have to say "yes" to every request made of me in order to be a good teacher and colleague. As I began to separate my self-worth from my performance on the job, I started to let go of the "college professor" identity and rediscover my identity in Christ.

Over the years I have been tackling that Can-Change List, slowly but surely. I have been re-introducing hobbies back into my life after letting them go based on the excuse that I didn't have the time to do anything for myself. I am trying to have more fun with Ann and the kids, laughing more, playing games more, and enjoying their company more. I am learning to live more in the moment rather than in the past or, more likely for me, in the future. I can't change the past or predict or control the future, but I can live, love, and be happy in the present.

...and the wisdom to know the difference.

This chapter has been largely about the wisdom to know the difference between what belongs on the Can-Change List and what needs to remain on the Cannot-Change List. This wisdom starts with a biblically sober judgment of our lives, honestly reflecting on the past and present, and assigning responsibility where it actually belongs. We must pray for serenity to accept the things on our Cannot-Change List, especially those from the past or that involve changing another person. We have to earnestly petition the Lord to fill us with courage to face down our Can-Change List, and with his help, to begin changing what we can and should change, one step at a time. Serenity, courage, and wisdom are deep spiritual gifts that come from the Creator himself, and He earnestly desires to give them to us (Matthew 7:7-8, James 1:5, Philippians 4:6-7).

In the coming chapters, we will unpack some of the most important lessons I have learned through sober judgment:

- Too many changes all at once can be overwhelming.
- My crazy-busy lifestyle was killing me – and it was my own fault.
- I tend to set myself up for disappointment with unfair, unrealistic, and unbiblical expectations.
- And possibly most importantly of all, I had bought into a pack of lies about life, God, myself, and other people.

While my struggles may not look exactly like yours, this is the kind of work that needs to be done to untangle the mess each of has made out of our lives. So, take a deep breath, let it out slowly, and let's dig in.

TRUE OR FALSE

Identifying and Challenging Harmful Self-Talk

"There is no voice more influential in your life than your own,
because no one talks to you more than you do."
Paul Tripp, *Lost in the Middle*[1]

Honest personal reflection is impossible if we don't believe the truth about ourselves and our situation. What we say to ourselves matters. If we tell ourselves the truth, we will eventually come to believe the truth. However, if we fill our heads with lies, then lies we will believe.

It would seem that I had been lying to myself for a very long time.

When I was lying in bed, too weak to move, staring at the ceiling and shaking all over, I just wanted to feel normal again. I found myself with countless long hours on my hands and nothing to do but think. When your mind isn't right, thinking isn't always the best thing for you. I wondered how God could let this happen to me. What had I done to have angered Him? Or had He just given up on me finally? There were times I found myself making a list of all my past sins and all the sins that I still struggle with today. I know that my sins have all been forgiven, that I have been washed white as snow, that the blood of Christ covers all my sin and that now when God sees me He sees only holiness. I also know that my daily life does not consist completely of holiness. Had God just finally had enough of my shenanigans and abandoned me?

Psychologists call the lies we believe "cognitive distortions." When we are first born, we think in abstractions; we think in feelings, images, and sensations. Very quickly, we begin to learn that the combination of sounds that form what we call words can make it so much easier for us to communicate all these abstractions. Before long, our thought processes are dominated not by abstractions and concepts but by words that represent them. We each have an inner monologue that is almost constantly running. If you don't believe me, put this book down, close your eyes, and try clearing your mind of words. How long can you go without words floating across your consciousness? If you're really good, you might be able to go five, six, or maybe seven seconds, but as long as our brains are going, words are flowing.

Many of our ideas about ourselves come from the words our parents used as they spoke to us and about us. If your parents were harsh and critical, then you very well may be harsh and critical towards yourself. If your parents were gentle, kind, and patient, then it's very likely that you speak to yourself in a similar tone.

- You are smart.
- You will never amount to much.
- You are special.
- You are a failure.
- You are valuable.
- You are not lovable as you are.
- You have incredible potential.
- You are a burden to me.
- You are trustworthy.
- You can't handle life's challenges.

The messages we received by observing their actions are often overlooked in our adult life. You mother may have never told you that you are unworthy of love and acceptance, but her behavior may have said that very thing. We need to learn to decode not only the overt messages in our heads, but also those that are hiding beneath the surface, ones that we ascertained by experience.

Our parents aren't the only ones who spoke into our young lives and shaped our inner monologues. After about age six, for most of us, our teachers spent a good part of the day with us, shaping our self-conception by speaking to us and about us. If those teachers believed in you, you may use language that reflects self-belief. If your teachers only tore you down or made you feel like a failure, then those old recordings of shame and unworthiness may still be playing in your head.

Besides our parents and teachers, many other people have shaped the words and concepts in our minds throughout our lifetimes. Friends, romantic interests, pastors, and even people we don't know gave us language with which to think about ourselves.

IT WOULD SEEM THAT I HAD BEEN LYING TO MYSELF FOR A VERY LONG TIME.

Although my parents divorced when I was quite young, I never doubted that they loved us kids. In fact, they often expressed words of admiration, love, and acceptance and gave us the confidence to try new things. While I am sure that their divorce early in my life has affected my sense of security somehow, I have no blame for my parents for the words they used to help me become who I am today.

Not everyone, however, had such kind and affirming words for me. In my early school years, through fourth grade, I was just one of the kids. I had my group of friends, and everyone seemed to get along reasonably well. I wasn't aware of social cliques. I didn't know who the cool kids were, and if I didn't fit in, I didn't know it. All that changed in fifth grade when we moved from my hometown in the suburbs to a nearby city where I was the new kid. The neighborhood was a bit rough, and that was reflected in the school. The teachers were excellent, looking out for us kids and doing all they could to teach us right from wrong. However, many of these kids came from tough family situations of their own, situations where words and actions spoke expectations that could not be met and disappointment from which one could not easily recover.

One such kid was Benny Columbo. Benny befriended me almost immediately when I arrived at the new school, but it didn't take long for an ugly side to emerge. Benny wanted to hang out with me as friends, but he also wanted to be able to push me around and make me feel small the way his harsh, hard-drinking dad pushed him around and made him feel small. And Benny's behavior towards me was even worse when some of the cool kids were around, the kids he hoped were his friends. Anytime I displeased Benny, he would threaten me by saying, "You're dead after school." Being that he was a full foot taller than me and had a little preteen mustache going, I believed him. There were many days at school that I couldn't focus, because all I could think about was the bus ride home and what might happen when we got off the bus. Most of the time, however, we would get off the bus and simply go home. Sometimes Benny would even say, "Hey, do you want to come play football today?" Or he would invite me to the local bowling alley where we would play Pac-Man and Space Invaders. Part of me, the part that needed a friend in this new town, wanted to accept his invitation. But part of me knew that this wasn't how friendship was supposed to be.

In both his words and his actions, Benny told me that I was unworthy of friendship, common decency, and even safety. He told me that I wasn't much of a man and that I wouldn't turn out to be anyone worthy of respect. He told me that I should be ashamed of myself.

Although I heard these messages nearly forty years ago, I find that some part of me still believes them.

After sixth grade, I moved back to my hometown, but to a new house in a much rougher part of the city. I began attending Catholic school, not because we were Catholic, but because of the excellent academics and the safer environment they provided relative to the local public schools. But I learned that middle-class Catholic kids can have rough family lives as well, and can be just as mean towards new kids as anyone else. My junior high years were a little better, but I was still the new kid, the small kid, the smart kid, the one who didn't fit in, the easy target. It wasn't until high school that I finally found the freedom to begin separating myself from that old person that had so easily been targeted by bullies. By then, a lot of damage had been done to my self-image and to the words I would use for many decades to come to speak to and about myself.

Well into middle age, I am only now beginning to untangle the complicated web of truths, half-truths, and outright lies that have formed much of my self-concept. Probably the most damaging of these have been the shaming statements that I am not enough, that I am unworthy of good friends, unworthy of love and acceptance. Shaming voices like these do us no good whatsoever. Guilt, the idea that I have done something wrong or bad, can at least motivate me to action. Guilt can be remedied by correcting the situation, by adjusting my behavior. Shame, on the other hand, simply condemns me by saying not that I have *done* something bad, but that I *am* something bad. Not only is this an outright lie, it is entirely unhelpful. If I call myself a loser, what action can I take to remedy the situation? But if I honestly acknowledge that I have a sin problem, or that I have a history of leaving tasks unfinished, or that I have bad eating habits, then I have something I can work on. Shame, however, is useless and only drags me down.

I first recognized that my worthiness, my worth as a human being, was in doubt in my own mind during a Sunday morning church service. During worship, we declare the worth of God. At one point I felt moved to lift my hands as a sign of adoration and submission to God, but quickly a voice in my head said, "Put your hands down, Dave. You are not worthy of worshiping this holy God." I sat down immediately, tears in my eyes, shocked, and wondering where that voice came from. Up until that time, I didn't think shame was a part of my struggle. Obviously, it is.

At the heart of shaming self-talk is the issue of our worthiness. Shaming statements make us believe that we are unworthy of love and acceptance because we are not perfect. This kind of self-defeating self-talk keeps us from building meaningful friendships. It keeps us stuck in unhealthy and even abusive relationships. We become unwilling to be vulnerable or to take any risks. Increasingly, we withdraw to the safety of our own minds and our own houses, never venturing out because we believe ourselves unworthy – or incapable – of good results.

Shaming statements sound ridiculous when spoken out loud:

- I am no good.
- There are no solutions for my problems.
- I am defective at my very core.
- I am a hopeless case.
- I am inadequate for the task.
- I am hopeless, worthless.
- Everything is my fault.
- I'd be better off dead.
- My friends and family would be better off if I was dead.
- I can't do this.
- I deserve this.
- No one could love me if they really knew me.

But speaking these shaming statements out loud is exactly what we need to do. Brené Brown, a shame researcher and author, tells us that naming our shaming statements is the first and most important step to building shame resilience.[2] If we can identify the lies that we've come to believe, and have the courage to share them with a trusted friend, we can begin to take the power away from the words. We become empowered to reality check the messages, to challenge them to prove themselves to be true. We can then begin to replace them with more truthful, more accurate, and more helpful statements. We must have courage, Brown tells us, to own our shame-filled struggles, without denying or hiding from them, and to face them head on. Only then will we begin to win the battle of words.

AT THE HEART OF SHAMING SELF-TALK IS THE ISSUE OF OUR WORTHINESS.

For some of us, shame is the very glue that holds together our anxiety or depression. If we can identify it, challenge it, and replace it with truthful and helpful self-talk, we can begin to dismantle the seemingly overwhelming forces of our mental and emotional health struggles.

Outright lies might possibly be the easiest kind of self-deception for us to recognize. For example, we might tell ourselves that no one could ever possibly love us because we believe that we are too broken, flawed, and damaged. Or we convince ourselves that all of our problems can be traced back to the hurtful, thoughtless words and actions of other people: "It's all their fault. I am a victim in this. There is nothing I can do about it." When spoken out loud, it's hard to believe sometimes that we would ever buy into these lies. But believe we do. In fact, the blatant, ridiculous, outrageous outright lies are sometimes the ones that dominate our thinking.

- This abusive relationship is all I deserve and all I can expect to find.
- I can be perfect if I try hard enough.
- God's love must be earned by my good behavior.
- I am a loser.
- I shouldn't have to change for my spouse.
- Saying "no" to other people's requests of me is just selfish.
- God is punishing me for my sins.
- My friends and family would be better off without me.
- I should be able to handle this.
- I know how this is going to end.

One of the outright lies I had believed was that I could do it all. I believed I could be an excellent teacher, an outstanding researcher, a dependable colleague, as well as perfect husband, the perfect dad, family handyman, the accountant, the small group leader, and anything else anyone else asked or needed me to be.

There were underlying lies behind this central lie that I could do and be it all. I had come to believe that I needed to be perfect to be acceptable, that I needed to have everyone's love and approval, and that my worth as a human being was determined by my performance in these various roles. I had bought into a whole set of lies that built one overarching deception that kept me running constantly, seeking approval and perfection: *you can and must do it all and do it perfectly.*

In *The Lies We Believe*, Dr. Chris Thurman says that the single most destructive lie of all is that we must be perfect.[3] So many of us fall into the trap of thinking that there is no room for mistakes. We set unrealistically high standards for ourselves, standards so high we wouldn't dare think of holding anyone else to them, yet we believe somehow that we should be capable of achieving such greatness. In fact, that word *should* comes up often in the minds of the perfectionist. I *should* be able to be everything for everyone at the highest of levels. I *should* be able to handle all of the stressors that life throws at me no matter what. I *should* have all the answers for all the questions from everyone who is counting on me. I have had to learn to drop the word "should" from my vocabulary. It is only a small step, but it has been an important one, one that calls to my attention when that lie begins to bubble up to the surface.

Another area where I struggled was with accurately assessing my challenges. The more stressed I became, the more I was likely to turn a molehill into a mountain. The more exhausted and overwhelmed I felt, the more likely I would take things personally that had nothing to do with me. The less competent and capable I felt, the more likely I was to look into my crystal ball and predict catastrophe from every new difficult situation. I began overgeneralizing. If I had a bad lecture in class, I told myself that I was a terrible teacher who could never get any better, and I should probably consider another line of work. If I said something insensitive to my wife, in my mind I was a monster who was heartless, cruel, and undeserving of her forgiveness and acceptance.

The effect of catastrophizing, overpersonalizing, and overgeneralizing my struggles was to convince me that I was a complete and utterly hopeless failure.

As I approached my breaking point, I found myself muttering "I can't do this." I sat in my truck stuck in traffic – *I can't do this*. I sat up late grading papers or preparing classes for the next day – *I can't do this*. I looked at my calendar and tried to plan how to fit everything in – *I can't do this*. Ann tells me that for a few months prior to my crash I had been saying, "I don't know how much longer I can do this." I was so overwhelmed that I couldn't distinguish the outright lies from the truth anymore. At that point, what I needed more than anything was a set of outside eyes who could look in on my situation and speak truth to me.

There are a variety of ways that we can lie to ourselves. We can blame ourselves for everything that's wrong in our lives, or we can just as easily put the blame 100% on other people and play the victim. We can be so blinded by our emotions that we begin to believe that what we feel is true. If we feel stupid when we make a mistake at work, then we must actually be stupid. If we feel like life has been unfair to us, then we begin to believe that we are destined in some way to be denied joy, peace, and love in our lives. We can assume that we know what other people are thinking about us, as if we have ESP. Or we believe, like I did, that we have a crystal ball that can see into the future and tell exactly just how badly things are going to turn out. The more we beat up on ourselves, the more we believe other people are beating up on us, the more our mental filter focuses on the negatives, ignoring the positives and even discounting anything good that does come our way.

Some of the most harmful statements we can make come in the form of all-or-nothing, black-and-white thinking. I am either perfect or I am a loser. Life is either perfectly fair or it is completely unfair. You are either my friend or my enemy. With this type of thinking, there is no gray area. There is only one way that is right and good and all else is a complete failure. Black-and-white thinking, like being a victim, can be very appealing. It takes the incredible complexities of our struggles and reduces them to only two options. I am either right or I am wrong. I am either good or I am bad. There is no room for alternative views or a work in progress. The result is that we often label ourselves irredeemably broken.

Of all the types of lies we buy into, the half-truths can be the most difficult to recognize and root out. When you make an actual mistake at work, and it costs you your job, it can be easy to believe the lie that you are a loser. After all, you did in fact screw up and you did lose your job because of it. But you see the problem here – you just

71

labeled yourself with a huge generalization: you made a mistake, it cost you your job, now you are applying the label "loser" to not only your work life but also to your very self. Half-truths look like the truth when we are not seeing clearly, but the damage of a half-truth is just as profound, hurtful, and self-destructive as an outright lie.

I WAS SO OVERWHELMED THAT I COULDN'T DISTINGUISH THE OUTRIGHT LIES FROM THE TRUTH ANYMORE.

What half-truths are you telling yourself that are holding you back? Here are a few that either I've told myself or others have shared with me:

- I am a failure as a parent.
- I am a failure as a husband.
- I am a terrible excuse for a Christian.
- I am not any good at this job.
- No one likes me or ever could like me.
- I will always be alone.

Do you see what is happening in each of these examples? Some small nugget of truth – a wayward child, a failed marriage, undefeated sin – blossoms into a full-blown accusation of unworthiness and failure. We ignore the truths about what we did well in our parenting, or how well we loved our spouse despite the conflicts, and all we can see is the failure. Until we are able to think clearly and base our assessments on the evidence, we will remain beholden to the influence of our old shame tapes and emotional responses.

My response to the chaos of all of my struggles and lies was to put on my blinders, put my nose to the grindstone, and do what I'd always been taught to do in tough times:

- Push through.
- Tough it out.
- Suck it up (buttercup!).
- Grow a spine.
- Get over it.
- Gut it out.
- Ride it out.
- Take it like a man.

These toxic, pithy expressions only serve to discount another human being's suffering. They are all different ways of saying that we need to muster the willpower to accept discomfort and suffering and simply do what needs to be done. When the trials we face are legitimately on the Cannot-Change List, then we do in fact need to learn to accept the circumstances. As we discussed in the previous chapter, though, far more of our circumstances belong on the Can-Change List rather than the Cannot-Change List. This means that when circumstances are unbearable, we often have choices in front of us that can change things for the better.

The other assumption in these trite, dismissive commands, is that we have endless will power which we can call on anytime and as often as necessary. Reality, however, is that we each have a finite store of fortitude to employ during the day. Some people, like trained soldiers, have more than others, but will power is not something that can be created on command. It must be cultivated over a lifetime so that it is available when it is really needed.

Telling someone to tough it out or push through hard times minimizes the pain they are experiencing, suggesting that it is easily resolved. It shows a lack of empathy and understanding for the difficulties many people face. The result, rather than motivation, is stigma and shame. Telling someone they need to push through a situation that is unbearable when the emotional reserves are unavailable to do so sends the message that the sufferer is inherently flawed or weak.

Telling a young mother who is struggling to get through each day with her children that she'd better suck it up because this is what she signed up for causes her to doubt her ability to be a good mom, filling her with a sense of shame.

Telling a businessman who is burnt out and exhausted from travel that he just has to push through and it will all be fine makes him question his career and even his manhood. The message is that "men are tough, and toughing it out is what we do. If life is too much for you, then you must not be very tough, and you must not be much of a man." What absolute nonsense.

But these were the things I had been telling myself for at least the last ten years.

- If I can just push through this semester, next year will certainly be much better.
- Once I have taught all of these courses a couple of times, my work life will become so much more manageable.
- This next raise should be enough for us to make it every month.

I told myself that my challenging situation was temporary, that soon everything would be made right and reasonable. How many times have you told yourself *As soon as_____ then I'll be happy*? Sometimes waiting for circumstances to change is a good idea, leading to patience and eventual improvement. Many times, however, nothing is going to change until we make it change by making new choices, sometimes hard choices, that will amend the situation. Most often we need to accept the things we cannot change or change the things we can – there is no wait until things change on their own.

An important step in living life honestly, viewing ourselves and our situations with sober judgment, involves identifying and challenging harmful self-talk. Many of the messages we play and replay on our mental tapes are simply not true, and others are only half-truths, jumbled up with lies that hurt us and hold us back. When the lies involve self-shaming language, we get stuck and have little hope of moving forward until we undo the ongoing damage.

In the coming chapters we will look closely at many of the ways of thinking and behavior that were most to blame for the breakdown of my mental health. Each of them began with me believing a lie.

You Can Keep the Change

The Stress of Major Life Changes

> "Nature's first green is gold,
> Her hardest hue to hold.
> Her early leaf's a flower;
> But only so an hour.
> Then leaf subsides to leaf.
> So Eden sank to grief,
> So dawn goes down to day.
> Nothing gold can stay."
> Robert Frost, "Nothing Gold Can Stay"[1]

When Aednat, the intake therapist, challenged me to do some deep reflection on the previous decade of my life, it didn't take long to see the pile of stressors and trials that had come my way and I had dutifully pushed aside. When she asked me how I grieved the death of my step-brother Jason, all I could manage to croak amidst the tears was, "there wasn't any time." That phrase seemed to characterize my life: no time to think, no time to grieve, no time to celebrate, no time to process anything. It felt as if I had simply pressed on from one event to the next at a hundred miles an hour, never slowing down, never bothering to try to understand it all.

It started with a series of major life changes that hit all at once in a matter of a few short weeks.

The first decade of our marriage was very good, enchanted we used to say. We spent our newlywed years in small-town Idaho and everything was coming up roses. For starters, we built some very close relationships with other people our age, many of whom were married and starting families just like we were. Something about a small town makes it easier to do life together. We shared meals together, studied the Bible together, watched each other's kids, painted one another's houses, went sledding together in the winter, and towed each other's cars when they died. We were an extended family to one another without all the family baggage.

If you've ever visited Idaho, you know that the landscape is second to none. Big rivers and small streams cut across wheat and potato farms and open ranch land, while tremendous mountain ranges frame nearly every view. With over thirty-five hundred miles of rivers (second only to Alaska in the US), it is a fly-fisherman's paradise. We fished, camped, and hiked as much as we could with young children.

After graduate school, I got a good job and we bought our first house, a beautiful 1950s ranch-style home with twenty-four hundred square feet, more than enough space for our growing family. We were away from our parents and siblings, so we had to learn to create our own traditions, especially around the holidays. We cooked our first Thanksgiving turkeys and cut our first Christmas trees in the local national forests. Our nine years in Idaho could only be described as idyllic.

After a few years in Idaho Falls, Ann and I both began to feel a call to work with college students full time. We had been leading a ministry through our church specifically for young people in their late teens and early twenties, some of whom were attending college and others who had begun careers or were still sorting out their next steps. We met weekly for Bible study, fellowship, and accountability. We became a small family with those friends, spending much of our free time with them watching movies or camping together. Our hearts were being shaped by this group of young people in ways that would set the course of our work and ministry for many years to come. But the Lord soon called us to a climate and culture about as opposite to rural Idaho as you can get.

When I first became aware that the Lord was calling me into ministry as a college professor, I prayerfully submitted applications to schools of all shapes and sizes: small Christian colleges, enormous state-run universities, and everything in between. I covered the US map pretty thoroughly, too, including institutions in the northeast, the south, the Midwest, the Northwest, and the Southwest. In all, I submitted nearly two dozen applications, blanketing the country and knocking on as many doors as I could. My vision for what this ministry would look like was still in its infancy and I didn't want to limit my options, the Lord's options for our next step as a family by being overly selective. So, I threw as many hats into as many rings as I felt I could manage.

Of the more than twenty applications I submitted, I interviewed at two institutions. The first was a state college in the south. The mild Tennessee weather in January was a welcome break from the harsh, sub-zero winter I left behind as my plane took off from the Idaho Falls Regional Airport. The people were laid back and warm, just as I had always heard southerners would be. The interview went very well, but something was missing. It seemed like my would-be colleagues viewed this work as just a job. They did what was needed to teach the students, but no one was interested in doing research in their area of specialty or getting involved in the students' lives. They had all chosen to be textbook teachers, simply explaining what they read about in the textbooks rather than remaining active in scholarly work so that they could teach from a place of knowledge and experience. The level of investment in students wasn't what I was looking for.

The next interview that was offered to me seemed highly serendipitous. My undergraduate alma mater invited me to interview for a faculty position in their biology department. When I left that beautiful campus nine years before, I assumed I was saying farewell to a place that had shaped me in life-altering, eternity-altering ways. If you are interested in a more detailed description of how I came to Christ, you can read it in Appendix D. For now, suffice it to say that I entered Point Loma Nazarene College as an agnostic, antagonistic towards Christians who I saw as simple-minded. I left three years later, committed to living my life for Jesus. Needless to say, this institution means a lot to me.

When I pinged my former biology professor at PLNU (it had since attained university status), he let me know that they were beginning a search for someone with expertise in either microbiology or botany. At his urging, I applied and much to my delight I was asked to visit and interview. If I was excited about the weather in Tennessee in January, San Diego in February felt as close to heaven as I could imagine!

The day we returned to Idaho Falls from the interview, the Dean of the College of Arts and Sciences called with a job offer. We had a big decision to make. The cost of living in Idaho Falls was a fraction of that in San Diego, and the paycheck from my government research job was nearly double what PLNU could pay me. The numbers just didn't add up. With three young children and a spouse committed to staying home with them for the first several years, how would we pay the bills? Would we be living in poverty, highly educated missionaries living in an American vacation destination? The math wasn't adding up, but we both kept coming back to the vision and mission of the university. We felt like this was a place where we could meld career and calling into a vocation, a ministry to young people during some of the most tumultuous and critical years of their lives. We said yes.

Experts say that major life changes, such as those associated with a move, can be highly stressful, even when those changes are joyful and bring happiness.[2] For example, moving entails new living conditions – new house, new neighborhood, new commute – all known to be very stressful. Changing cities also involves changing jobs, even if you are sticking with the same company. Job changes are even more stressful when they include new responsibilities or an entirely new line of work. Moving can be an exciting opportunity for a fresh start, but we have to acknowledge that moving brings a considerable amount of stress to our lives as well.

Maybe you're thinking, "C'mon Dave, what's so hard about moving? People move all the time."

MAJOR LIFE CHANGES CAN BE HIGHLY STRESSFUL, EVEN WHEN THOSE CHANGES ARE JOYFUL AND BRING HAPPINESS.

True, moving isn't all that uncommon in American culture. In fact, a 2013 Gallup poll found that 24% of Americans had changed cities or regions within the past five years.[3] We are undoubtedly a very mobile generation, but just because everyone is doing it doesn't mean it is easy on us. It all comes down to trade-offs: what benefits am I getting, and what is it costing me? This kind of assessment is essential if we are to ever live honestly with ourselves.

In a matter of just a few months we would say goodbye to our church family, my job, our first house, and the beautiful Idaho land, people, and culture that we had grown to love so much. We bid adieu to four seasons, pine forests, and summer thunderstorms. As we watched the state that had become home to us for the past decade disappear in our rearview mirrors, we walked away from everything we knew as a married couple and headed into a new adventure.

Even though Ann was born in California and I had already lived in San Diego through my college years, we were in for a real culture shock. We moved from a rural town of 57,000 residents – which, incidentally, is the second largest city in the state of Idaho – to a vast region with over three million people. It was a veritable sea of humanity adjacent to an even greater ocean of souls, Los Angeles. The city of San Diego alone contains more people than the entire state of Idaho, and the state of California boasts a larger population than that of the entire nation of Canada!

The population density in southern California is staggering, and when juxtaposed with a decade of life in Idaho, I was overwhelmed. In Idaho, I could get on the only freeway in the area and within five minutes I was in rolling fields of barley and open ranch land. San Diego traffic is another story. Here, I can drive for forty-five minutes and, on a good day, get to my office alongside millions of my fellow travelers. The crowded freeways point to crowded stores, restaurants, parking lots, schools, you name it. Even though I had spent my college years in San Diego, I was a different person now. I was a husband, father, and Idahoan. This was going to take some getting used to.

Another adjustment that must be made with a big move involves leaving old friends behind and making new friends. Leaving a place where everybody knows your name, where you can't go to the grocery store without bumping into a friend, to a place where you do not know a single soul can be a very lonely experience. The loneliness we both felt in the first year or two made us question our decision to come here. We literally drove away from our entire support system: all of the people we depended on to get through the tough times, the people we celebrated the victories with, the people we most wanted by our side as we stepped into the unknown. Instead we were adrift, no one to turn to but one another for encouragement and companionship.

Similarly, leaving a church with established relationships and finding a new one, one whose mission and methods you can get behind, can be very difficult. We spent several months "church shopping" around San Diego, which is home to literally hundreds of Christian churches. When we first arrived, the number of options for churches to visit made our heads spin. If we're honest, the whole "church shopping" experience is not particularly good for our spiritual lives. When we're shopping around for a new church to attend, we play the role of the critic and look for reasons to label a church as the wrong one for us. We think and behave more like we're car shopping than looking for a community where we can grow and serve.

Another considerable challenge people face when moving to big American cities is the cost of living increase. Even if I hadn't taken a substantial pay cut, the sticker shock of housing prices in the area would be enough to send many people packing. To put it into perspective, the house we eventually purchased in San Diego was smaller and needed more TLC than our house in Idaho. It also cost precisely five times the price of our house in Idaho Falls! Even with a sizable deposit, we were still left with a mortgage that was more than two times what we were on the hook for in Idaho and a paycheck that was about half of our previous income. *What were we thinking?!*

It will come as no surprise to you that our finances were a major stressor in our lives for the decade leading up to my crash. In addition to a significant pay cut coupled with an astronomical increase in housing costs, I had spent eleven years accumulating student loan debt equal to a modest mortgage in Idaho. It wasn't clear to me how we were going to make this work financially. Less than a year into the new job, I was already considering what our next move was going to be. I didn't see a path forward that was financially viable.

Student loan debt is increasing at an alarming rate in the US, stressing out students and parents alike. As of 2017, Forbes reported a total indebtedness of $1.31 trillion for student loans, with over 44 million borrowers.[4] That's an average of almost $30,000 per borrower. I was on the hook for considerably more than that since I had attended a private college as well as more than five years of graduate school. Starting our young marriage with that sort of debt hanging over our heads caused more than its fair share of stress.

At some point all debts must be paid. Like many college students, I assumed that I'd have a job straight out of college that would be more than adequate for quickly paying off my student loans. Reality is, however, that the years after college often come with many of their own expenses and adventures like marriage, kids, and a mortgage; starting pay, even for college graduates, isn't always as high as we might have been led to believe. My own adventures meant paying the minimum required amount on my loans for 17 years, finally making my last payment just as my oldest child was entering her senior year of high school. I cannot overstate the stress that financial burden, accumulated through a combination of necessity, naiveté, and discontentment, placed on my wife and me for the first two decades of our marriage. Along with other financial struggles, the specter of seemingly endless student loan debt certainly contributed to the degradation of my mental and physical health over the last decade.

In a very short period of time, Ann and I had experienced some of the most disruptive changes life has to offer. We moved from our home and friends in Idaho Falls to San Diego where we had to begin again. Not only was it difficult to say goodbye to people and a familiar life in Idaho, we had to find a new church, make new friends, and adjust to a completely different culture in southern California. That move alone, along with the associated changes and adjustments, would have been enough to introduce significant stress into our lives.

As it turned out, the move was only half of the story.

Possibly the biggest change – at least for me – was in my work. I had it pretty good as a postdoctoral fellow working for the US Department of Energy in Idaho. We lived four easy miles from the laboratory, so I could have breakfast at home in the mornings with Ann and the kids. Nearly every day they would bring lunch to me and we would spend half an hour together, eating and relaxing. Security was strict at the facility where I worked, so we ate our lunches outside when the weather was nice and in the car with the heater running in the colder months. Every other Friday was a mandatory day off (yes, you read that correctly: *mandatory*), so I had frequent three-day weekends. Research funding was easy to come by through in-house sources. I traveled every couple of months for a few days at a time to science conferences, field sites, and research meetings where I stayed in fancy hotels and ate in excellent restaurants for every meal. Maybe best of all, I rarely felt the need to bring any work home with me in the evenings or on weekends.

Compare that with the life of a new college professor at a Christian liberal arts university. When I arrived on campus a couple weeks before fall semester classes began I was handed course titles and the catalog descriptions. No curriculum, no textbook, no syllabus. Up until that point it hadn't occurred to me that a college professor has to deliver about forty-five hours of lectures for each class he or she is teaching in a given semester. And I was teaching two courses along with a few lab sections – at least those were already prepared and all I had to do was learn them and figure out how to best explain them to the students. But creating a course syllabus, all of the learning objectives, activities, and assessments, along with forty-five hours of classroom content, was a real shock to my naïve system.

During my first semester, we lived in a two-bedroom apartment on campus. Ann and I, along with four-year-old Sydney, two-year-old Ryan, and two-month-old Josh, shared less than nine hundred square feet. We also shared walls with the college students in neighboring apartments and the young family upstairs (who quickly became some of our closest friends). As busy and overwhelmed as we were, we hardly had the brain capacity to appreciate the west-facing ocean view from the second-floor living room sliding glass door – a view of sunsets over the Pacific Ocean that we knew we'd never have again after buying a house of our own.

Living on campus, just a five-minute walk from the office, was a mixed blessing. On the one hand, it was easy to pop in for lunch with Ann and the kids, or meet them for a short midday walk around campus. There was no commute to wear me down or eat up precious daylight. On the other hand, it was far too easy to work continuously, never really separating from the job even when I was at home. My routine that first semester was to wake up around five a.m., have a shower and breakfast, and work on that day's teaching activities: lectures or labs. Sometime mid-morning I would walk to the science building and work a full day, meeting with students and faculty, delivering lectures, creating and grading assignments, teaching labs, and eventually getting started on the next day's order of business. After dinner, back at the apartment, it was back to the books and lectures and labs in preparation for the next day. I usually crashed around midnight, in time for a few hours of sleep and then started the routine all over again the next day. Strong coffee became my constant companion.

At best, most days I was only twenty-four hours ahead of the students in terms of reading the textbook and making sure I understood the material well enough to explain it. Some days I was only a few hours ahead of them. More than once I was finishing my lectures just minutes before heading to the classroom, or even finishing them in the classroom as the students filed in. The pace was frenetic and the pressure to be prepared was intense.

THE MORE AMBITIOUS AND DRIVEN A PERSON IS, THE MORE DIFFICULT IT IS TO KNOW WHEN TO STOP.

The pressure to be "on," like an actor on stage or a live TV or radio personality, is intense in the world of college teaching. Multiple times each day a college professor has to show up to the classroom or laboratory, prepared with something to say. I had disturbing dreams during that first year of walking into a classroom having not prepared for the day and having no clue what to say or do for the next hour. Usually, I was just wearing my underwear. That fear is enough to make a new professor stay up late into the night or wake up pre-dawn to prepare for class. Being unprepared at class time was not an option.

It didn't help my situation that, like many of my colleagues, I tend to be highly ambitious. When I see a better way to teach a topic or an activity that is going to help my students grasp a difficult concept, I can't help but put in the effort to go the extra mile, even when it means losing sleep to do so. Any teacher can attest to the fact that this profession will take anything and everything one is willing to give to it. Like an artist creating a piece of art, it is difficult for a teacher to know when enough is enough when preparing a lecture or class activity. And the more ambitious and driven a person is, the more difficult it is to know when to stop.

The result for me was seventy or more hours per week and complete physical, mental, and emotional exhaustion. All I could do was cling to the promise of my colleagues that it would get better with time, that I would create a database of lectures and activities to draw from in the future, and that my life might possibly, eventually return to something that looked almost normal.

In Chapter 2 I briefly told you about my brother-in-law, Sam, and his eighteen-month battle with leukemia. Sam lost his fight and went home to be with the Lord just a few weeks before our move back to

California. With all of the logistics of the move, it was conveniently difficult to spend time mourning and processing Sam's death. To be sure, we were hurting. We missed our little brother. It seemed so unfair for God to allow someone so young, so full of life and promise, to be stolen from us just before graduating from high school. We were faced with the "why" questions that everyone asks when a loved one dies too soon (according to our timeline and expectations). Making those "why" questions more poignant was the fact that Sam was a passionate, committed follower of Jesus. He played in the church worship band and was hoping to go to college to study Worship Arts. This was a young man unquestionably on track to accomplish great things for God and His kingdom. *Why would God allow such a person to die? If Sam had to die for some eternal purpose, why couldn't he have died quickly and painlessly? Why did he have to suffer for so long with leukemia before the Lord took him home?*

These are all legitimate questions, questions everyone who grieves the loss of a loved one has the right to ask, questions that God expects and can handle. But rather than allowing myself to feel the pain and think those tough questions, processing them with prayer and the support of friends and family, I poured myself into the move from Idaho to California and all it demanded of me. It was a convenient escape from the grief. This way I didn't have to face tough questions that I wasn't sure my young Christian faith could handle. It turns out that when we hide from grief, it doesn't somehow naturally resolve itself. The old adage that time heals all wounds isn't entirely accurate. Unprocessed grief, stuffed deep and ignored for years, eventually comes back to the surface in painful and unexpected ways. Grief will not be denied its time in the spotlight.

In addition to leaving our friends and home in Idaho and dealing with the loss of our youngest sibling, we had a new addition to the family. Josh was born just after Sam passed away and only a matter of weeks before we moved back to California. Josh is an amazing young man, full of energy and intensity from the very beginning. We used to say that he was naturally caffeinated. From his first day *ex utero* his eyes were open so wide you could see the whites all around the iris, like he had just had a double espresso from Dutch Bros and was ready to go. He napped very little for a newborn, and in fact didn't sleep through the night – for the very first time – until he was two years old. To this day, Josh sleeps hard, wakes up early, and is immediately ready to take on the world with gusto. We wouldn't change him for the world.

GRIEF WILL NOT BE DENIED ITS TIME IN THE SPOTLIGHT.

Most couples would agree that a baby is a blessing, but even blessings can cause stress. Adding a member to the family, be it through natural childbirth or adoption, is both wonderful and trying. Josh has been one of the most wonderful things to happen to our family, but between the lack of sleep and the process of getting to know a new human being with all of his quirks and needs, we were stretched pretty thin.

Any major life change – marriage, divorce, moving, buying a home, changing jobs, having a baby or adopting a child, among countless others – brings with it a certain amount of stress, even when the change is exciting and welcome. When life conspires to hit us with numerous major life changes all at once, we can quickly find ourselves in deep trouble. Without the right attitude and good coping skills, we can easily become overwhelmed. My coping strategy of choice was to minimizing the challenges for as long as possible and keeping my nose to the grindstone. I tried to push through because that's what I thought I was supposed to do. But minimizing our struggles and pushing through or toughing it out are not coping strategies at all – they are merely ways of denying the reality we are facing, and unless we are willing to make some serious changes, we will eventually crash.

Sometimes we are in denial of our dangerous and harmful reality simply because we are too busy to take notice. When we fill every waking moment with doing, we leave no time for processing. In the next chapter, we will talk about how my crazy busy lifestyle contributed to my mental and emotional collapse.

CRAZY BUSY

The High Cost of Trying to Do It All

"Busyness does not mean you are a faithful or fruitful Christian. It only means that you are busy, just like everyone else."
Kevin DeYoung, *Crazy Busy*[1]

In the days and weeks and months leading up to my crash, a typical day for me started at 6:30 a.m. and didn't slow down until 9 or 10 p.m. I left myself precious little time to think, process, recover, reset my brain, exercise my body, pray, read the Bible, or any other healthy coping strategy. Maybe you can relate to the feeling of not enough hours in the day. Sometime we can push through and make this work for a little while, but this lifestyle just isn't sustainable. Something has to give. For me, it was my health.

Imagine that your capacity for stressors, busyness, struggles, and challenges in life is a cup. Maybe your cup is a little coffee mug with the face of a kitten, or maybe it's a gigantic Big Gulp. The size of your cup is determined partly by genetics, partly by your life experiences – some nature, some nurture. If you are like many of us, your job demands quite a bit of the space in your cup. Maybe your cup is already 75% full because of your work responsibilities. When you get home at night, the kids need help with homework, the dishes need to be done, and dinner is not going to cook itself.

Busy is busy, and our time and emotional resources are finite.

How much of that remaining space in your cup is taken up by these routines, these necessary things in life? Is there any space left over for other things, activities that may require your time or mental energy? Is there any room in your cup for self-care activities, things that restore your energy and sanity? For many of us, the answer is no.

As I reflected on the previous decade of my life leading up to the crash, I couldn't help but notice the intense pace I had taken on. Not only was I working longer hours, I now had an hour-long commute in heavy traffic. A recent study done by the Texas A & M Transportation Institute found that the average working American spends thirty-eight hours per year stuck in traffic.[2] While that sounds like a big chunk of life to dedicate to driving back and forth to work, at eight to ten hours per week, my annual average falls more along the lines of four to five hundred hours! I often find that I leave campus excited to see Ann and the kids, thinking about some project I have in the shop or an activity with the family. By the time I get home an hour later, I just want to sit on the couch in silence and veg out.

But, of course, I can't afford to veg out. There is dinner to be made (or helped with), homework to be done, basketball practice to get one kid to and track practice to pick another one up from. Dishes need to be done, the broken gate in the fence needs to be repaired, and the pastor has called a meeting of the church elders. There are Bible studies to lead and others to attend, groceries to shop for, weeds to pull from the yard, and a hurting friend to listen to. My cup was already full from the basics of everyday life, and anything else just caused it to spill over.

Keeping up with the basics – job, school, home – already taps us for just about all we are worth. We still say yes to countless other requests on our time, good things that could provide a nice diversion from routine responsibilities. Things like helping at church, attending a Bible study, or coaching the kids' soccer team. We add busyness to our already busy lives and it's no wonder that we are exhausted. I hadn't yet learned that being too busy with good things is still being too busy.

In my case, it didn't take much beyond the routine to push me into being overwhelmed, to cause my cup to spill over. My routine activities were already time- and energy-consuming, yet I found myself saying yes to many requests of my time, all good things, worthy of my time and resources, activities that would use my gifts and talents to pour into the lives of people. But busy is busy, and our time and emotional resources are finite. We all need some wiggle room, some headspace in the cup to leave room for everything else in life without the threat of spilling over.

Pastor Kevin DeYoung, quoted at the beginning of this chapter, wrote a short and powerful book about this problem. He called it, appropriately, *Crazy Busy*.[1] In it, he not only makes the case that we are vastly under-effective in life because we have embraced the crazy busy culture, but he helps us to understand the underlying heart issues that lead us to such a broken place.

DeYoung, a successful pastor, speaker, and author, confesses, "I've been too busy to pursue God with my whole heart, soul, mind, and strength."[1] One of the most insidious problems with crazy busy is that it gives us a false sense of accomplishment. Crazy busy makes us feel like we are being productive, but more often than not we are just running around trying to keep up with everything on our plates. Crazy busy has a way of stealing from us the most important and life-giving activities in exchange for what amounts to little more than filler. I want to pursue the real substance. The world can keep its filler.

As just an example, listen to the words and phrases mothers chose to describe themselves in a recent Barna study:[3]

- Overcommitted (56%)
- Dissatisfied (with work/life balance) (62%)

- Tired (70%)
- Stressed out (80%)

From these numbers it seems fair to say that our moms are really struggling to get through each day. And you know the old adage: If momma ain't happy, ain't nobody happy!

We've even dragged our kids into a crazy busy lifestyle. We sign them up for every sport imaginable and shout at them as if their entire future depended on this at-bat. Many schools are giving kindergartners daily homework and in our school district they've shortened summer break to only eight weeks. They take piano lessons and work with a batting coach and stay up until midnight trying to get their homework done, all for the purpose of... what? Richard Swenson, author of the book *Margin*, hits the nail on the head when he says, "Our children lay wounded on the ground, run over by our high-speed good intentions."[4] For many of us, this is a central part of the legacy we are leaving them. But why?

I had mindlessly adopted a crazy busy lifestyle. During therapy, my wife revealed that I had more than once said to her, "I don't know how much longer I can keep this up," a sure sign that my cup was full and beginning to spill over. I was overwhelmed, overcommitted, overstimulated, distracted, and irritable. I was going through life in a fog, never fully present, as I submitted to the tyrannical pace I had accepted as my lot in life. My cup was indeed beginning to spill over, but I was so busy that I didn't notice, not until I could no longer move. It wasn't until my body said "enough!" and shut down that I finally began to take notice of the unsustainable lifestyle I was living and the high price that I, and those around me, were paying for it.

We become crazy busy for many reasons.

For me, the first reason I had allowed myself to get crazy busy was my pride. When someone asked me how I was doing, my answer always somehow included a comment about how busy I was.

"Hey Dave, how's it going?"

"Oh, you know, doing my best to keep up," I'd say, shaking my head in false humility.

"Busy" had become a badge of honor. I was proud of being so busy because it meant, in my warped thinking, that I was important. I was like that person you see in the grocery store or the airport talking loudly on their cell phone about some business, emphasizing dollar amounts and making threats that show how powerful they are. If I was crazy busy, I must be in high demand and therefore indispensable to someone somewhere.

I'm not the first person to take pride in my busyness. I hear people talk about how busy they are all the time. We brag about how long our hours are at work, or how far we drive for the kids' sports competitions over the weekend, or all the improvement projects we have going on at home. Personalized license plates boast about being LWYS BSY, and plate frames tease, "I'm busy. Can I ignore you later?" Somewhere along the way we have decided that being busy is good and having any free time on our hands just means we're lazy or unimportant.

AVOIDANCE EVENTUALLY COMES BACK TO BITE US.

Related to pride, crazy busy often results from a need for affirmation. If we are not moving at a high rate of speed, if we are not accomplishing more and more for God, if we are not involved in every good endeavor, or if, heaven forbid, we are ever the least bit bored (gasp!), we do not receive the affirmation and personal validation from others that come from a crazy busy lifestyle. More than pride, I felt the need to be affirmed in my worth by other people who saw the busy things I was doing. And if it didn't come up in conversation, social media was always there to make sure at least a couple hundred people knew how hard I was going. My fragile ego needed to hear from others that I was OK in their eyes, and projecting a crazy busy life seemed to get the quickest results.

Many of us, myself included, use busyness as an avoidance technique. Life is hard, and processing the failures and stressors of the day is not fun, especially when your cup is already feeling full.

But the busier I could stay, the less deeply I had to dive into painful thoughts or confront my own shortcomings. I have come to realize, however, that thinking about, considering, and praying over stressors, both big and small, is an essential part of hitting the reset button and calming my frazzled nerves by putting the fight-or-flight response on hold. Every time we hit reset, it's like pouring out some of the stressors that are filling the cup, creating more headspace for the next round of challenges. Resetting our hearts and minds through prayerful processing of the day's – or week's, or year's – events is a key step in building resilience for future challenges (more on building resilience in later chapters).

I was staying crazy busy so that I didn't have to process it all. My cup was overflowing, and not in the good sense of God giving us His love, but in the sense of feeling entirely overwhelmed and outmatched by life. It was an avoidance method that many of us have adopted because we think that avoidance is much less painful than facing our demons, and I had mastered the technique.

Avoidance, however, eventually comes back to bite us. There is no such thing as permanent avoidance without paying a high price in our hearts, minds, and even our bodies. In his best-selling book, *The Body Keeps the Score*, psychiatrist Bessel van der Kolk makes a compelling case that trauma – similar in many ways to chronic stress – must be faced at some point or it will emerge as biological illness in the brain and/or body. "We have learned that trauma is not just an event that took place sometime in the past; it is also the imprint left by that experience on mind, brain, and body. This imprint has ongoing consequences for how the human organism manages to survive in the present."[5] Stress will, one way or another, eventually have its day in the spotlight.

We live in a fast-paced culture that is only getting faster. It seems like each generation feels like they have to do more and do it more quickly than the previous generation. If our parents worked fifty hours a week, then we have to work sixty. If our parents had two different employers over their careers, then we have to work for five different companies. If we played two sports then our kids should play four sports. Somehow the idea of progress has gotten jumbled up in our minds and we've confused it with busyness.

The pressure to be busy, or at least appear busy, is intense and comes from many directions. The idea of being bored, even for just a few minutes, has become loathsome to us, even shameful. What do you do when you're standing in line at the grocery store? If you're like many of us, you probably stare at your phone for those one hundred and twenty seconds. We'd rather kill time looking busy than looking around, risking the judgment of others, risking having to engage another human being in face-to-face conversation. We teach our kids to resist peer pressure to drink alcohol or engage in sexual activity, but we have not listened to our own words. While we might be able to recognize and resist peer pressures to do things that are clearly bad for us, we have bought hook, line, and sinker into the pressure to stay – or at least look – busy.

Part of the problem is that, in today's age of pocket technology, limitless communication, and easy transportation, opportunities to do good things are virtually endless. The sheer number of opportunities to serve at church, to participate in short-term mission trips, to volunteer with one non-profit or another, to play sports year-round, to do extra at work… the list goes on without any end in sight. Our natural inclination is to try to be involved in all of these great opportunities. DeYoung says, "because we *can* do so much, we *do* do so much."[1] What we need now more than ever are boundaries not just to protect us from harmful things but to guide us to the best of all the good things. We have to pick and choose – we simply can't have it all, not without mortgaging our personal well-being and that of our children in order to live the ever-expanding American dream.

Sometimes we violate our own boundaries, saying yes to things we simply cannot afford to add to our schedules, because we feel guilty. It can be excruciating to sit on a gift, knowing you could make a difference, but not doing so. If you have construction skills, the guilt of not volunteering when the church is looking for help remodeling the classrooms can be overwhelming. If you are a marriage counselor, seeing a need for a ministry to married couples in your church may make you feel like you have to step up and fill the void. Somewhere along the way many of us have been taught that if there is a need that we can fill, we have to be the ones to fill it. It has been said that 90% of the work in a church is accomplished by 10% of the people. I'm among that 10% that feels obligated to get the work done, all 90% of it.

Being responsible and dependable is admirable. Stepping up to sacrificially meet the needs of others is the road that Jesus calls us to walk. But one problem with letting guilt drive our activities rather than a cheerful heart is that those activities become a burden and we grow resentful. Resentment is one of those emotions that is powerful enough to dominate our thinking. It can keep us up at night, distract us from our blessings, and prevent us from spiritual growth. None of us can live a fruitful and productive life, one of meaning and purpose, one of peace and joy, under a dark cloud of resentment.

WE DEFER MUCH-NEEDED MAINTENANCE ON OUR HEARTS AND BODIES, THINKING THAT WE ARE TOO BUSY FOR SOMETHING SO SELFISH AS SELF-CARE.

Another problem with guilt-driven busyness is that we will tend to run ourselves into the ground until we are no longer any good to anyone. When we were younger, Ann and I had a Toyota Camry that was our workhorse. It got both of us to work and church and anywhere else we needed to go. We ran kids to play dates and doctor appointments. We shopped for groceries in that car and took long road trips to visit family in other states. One year I naively procrastinated getting the oil changed when it was due. *I am so busy, how can I spare the time? And besides,* I reasoned, *it's a Toyota, and everyone knows how well-made Toyotas are. It will be fine. I'll get the oil changed eventually, when life slows down a little.* Twelve months and twelve thousand miles later, the car started spitting and sputtering. I had run the engine dry of oil and the cylinders had pitted beyond repair. That engine was finished, and we were carless until we could get a new one.

Sadly, many of us do the same thing to ourselves. We defer much-needed maintenance on our hearts and bodies, thinking that we are too busy for something so selfish as self-care. But then we break down, like a car run into the ground. Then what are we good for? Without the ability to say no, even to perfectly good and reasonable requests, our engines are going to get fried, like my old Camry motor.

For many of us, there just aren't enough hours in the day to accomplish everything we've put on our to-do lists. Our cups are practically overflowing already, without worrying about the unexpected things that crop up every so often. The reasons we allow ourselves to become crazy busy are as diverse as we are, yet the effects are the same: stress, anxiety, depression, feelings of being overwhelmed, irritability, and ineffectiveness.

Restoring sanity to our crazy busy lives starts with confessing that we are finite beings, incapable of doing it all. In the next chapter we will unpack what is required to reclaim our lives from the tyrannical pace that many of us have accepted as our fate. When you're ready, turn the page.

FIGHTING BACK

Strategies for Slowing Down the Crazy Train

"Yes, I will lay down this frantic way of living. Yes, I will show up to the event that I've been invited to. This event, of course, is my life."
Shauna Niequist, *Present over Perfect*[1]

Every August, hundreds of starry-eyed eighteen-year-olds and their parents descend on our campus for New Student Orientation. They come with dreams of what the next four years will hold and expectations based on all they've heard from friends and seen on TV about college life. Many have worked extremely hard to get here and fully expect to have to step up their game to meet the high standards of college courses. For others, the road to college has been fairly smooth through studying occasionally if absolutely necessary, but mostly relying on their God-given intellect to carry them along to success. Sometimes students in this second category are in for a rude awakening in their first year at the university.

New Student Orientation weekend wraps up with words of encouragement and wisdom from current students and faculty in each student's chosen major department. Ironically, my role in this event for the past decade has been to give stern warnings about the importance of self-care during college. I warn them that mom and dad will no longer be there to get them out of bed on time or insist that they eat a healthy breakfast before class. Most professors won't offer extra credit to bail them out when they perform poorly on an exam or homework assignment. The stress and pressure created by the intense pace of college life, I advise, pushes all of us to our breaking points at some time or another. Students must begin taking responsibility for their own personal health. They need to eat well, get plenty of sleep, and exercise every day. They need to set limits on all of the extra-curricular activities they sign up for and make their schoolwork a high priority. At the same time, they need to invest in relationships, be part of a local church community, read the Bible every day, and seek help before they reach the point of no return. Work hard but pace yourselves, I implore them. This isn't summer camp, but neither is it prison camp. Find balance. Seek your identity in Christ, not academic success. In short, don't put self-care on hold, thinking college life is too busy to take care of yourself.

What a sham.

Apparently, I had all kinds of great thoughts and words to share with the incoming freshmen that I didn't believe enough to apply to my own life. If only I had been listening to myself!

When I speak to adults on this subject, many people argue that I must not understand their specific circumstances. If I did, they assert, I would know that there was no possible way on God's green earth that they could slow down this crazy life. It just isn't possible. Well, I'm not convinced. Until you abandon the lie (yes, it is a lie) that you have no control over the intensity of your life, nothing is going to change.

If you are willing to consider new attitudes and actions that could make a difference and give you some breathing room and more of the peace that Jesus promises is available to us, read on.

1. Confess you are finite.

So how do we beat back the attacks of crazy busy that threaten our families, our churches, and our own sanity? How do we get off this treadmill that has us running a million miles an hour but getting us nowhere? It starts with a simple confession. Say it with me: "I am finite. I do not have unlimited energy and time." Write it down on a bunch of sticky notes and post them everywhere you can. Repeat it often throughout the day until it becomes part of your worldview.

UNTIL WE BELIEVE THAT WE ARE FINITE AND SIMPLY CANNOT DO IT ALL, WE WILL CONTINUE TO TAKE ON TOO MUCH AND EXPERIENCE PAIN AND SUFFERING FOR IT.

When we get crazy busy, even though we think we are on top of the world by doing everything, we are really cheating all of the things we are trying to do by giving far less than 100% of ourselves to them. The math is simple. If I have $100, I can spend $1 on each of one hundred cheapo things at the dollar store, or I can buy two high-quality items from a specialty shop for fifty bucks each. What I can't do is buy one hundred high-quality items, not unless I over-spend and borrow money using my credit card. Then, just like over-spending my time and energy resources, the debt will eventually come due. With interest. Until we believe that we are finite and simply cannot do it all, we will continue to take on too much and experience pain and suffering for it.

2. Build margin into your life.

What we need, and what we are so clearly lacking, is room to breathe, think, and heal. We need time to process the challenges we face and grow from our mistakes. We need the space to enjoy life, not simply survive it. Richard Swenson calls this space "margin."[2]

"Margin… is having breath left at the top of the staircase, money left at the end of the month, and sanity left at the end of adolescence."

He argues that our lives are spiraling out of control because we are taking on too much, trying to do too many things. We have forfeited all margin in our lives and it has left us ineffective at work and in ministry, irritable and undependable at home, and entirely overwhelmed.

Besides making us less effective at the things we are trying to do, lack of margin leaves us unable to process and heal from life's pain. "We *must* have some room to breathe," Swenson writes. "We need freedom to think and permission to heal." He's not just talking about healing from traumatic events, although we certainly need time and space to deal with those; we also need time and space to think and heal from each day's stressors. We need to process not only the big events – the death of a loved one or the loss of a job – but also all the little events along the way. As I learned all too well, little stressors that are not processed can have the same effect as big traumas. Stress, it turns out, is cumulative, particularly if we do not hit reset frequently.

When our cups are filled to the brink with demands on our time and energy reserves, we have no capacity, no margin, for the unexpected. But life itself is filled with unexpected events: an illness, a surprise visit from a relative, a phone call from a friend needing support. As I write this chapter, our minivan is in the shop. The cooling fan had been blowing for fifteen or twenty minutes after it was turned off, and then yesterday it overheated. It is unrealistic for us to be shocked and surprised when the unexpected comes. We need to learn to take life's unpredictable turns in stride.

Not only does life have a way of blowing up our plans with unexpected visitors and cars breaking down, God reserves the right to interrupt our plans at any time He chooses to insert himself and His plans. In fact, you could make the argument that God's agenda for us should be primary and our own plans only realized if they fit into His "divine appointments." When we fill and overfill our schedules, we leave no wiggle room for such divine appointments. Undoubtedly, some "good works, which God prepared in advance for us to do" (Ephesians 2:10) are going undone because of the primacy of our crazy busy schedules.

Margin needs to become a priority if we are going to be available to respond to the Holy Spirit's leading. If we are going to fulfill our individual calling from God, we must remain available to Him and not overloaded and overwhelmed with our own busy schedules. We need to set clear boundaries, lines beyond which we will not venture, so that we can find rest as needed and be available to do the good works Paul speaks of in Ephesians 2.

We need to strategically plan for margin in our lives. And we need to value that down time, that headspace when we can rest and think and process all that has happened today, this week, this year.

3. Clarify your priorities.

If I asked you to make a list of the top five most important things in your life, what would you write down? Worshipping God? Encouraging character development in the kids? Investing in other people? What if you were tasked with creating a time budget by mapping out how you spend each minute of the day? How would that line up with your list of priorities?

When we try to do it all, we tend to neglect the most important things. At the very best, we do them poorly. My values were focused on God and family, but all my time and energy were going into career, home repairs, and kids' activities (which is a different beast than what I have in mind when I say that family is an important value to me). I was trying to do it all, but in the end I could only do some of it, and I did that portion very poorly.

Crazy busy is particularly damaging to our spiritual life. Living life at a frenetic pace has the effect of lowering the priority of spiritual disciplines such as daily Bible study, worship, and prayer. When I have sped through the week and saved all of my rest time for Sunday, I make excuses to skip church. When my kids' activities schedule runs the family, I leave no margin for participating in a couples' Bible study with Ann or helping the Amor team build homes across the border in Tijuana. If I'm honest, my busy schedule becomes an excuse for not doing many of the harder things that I claim to hold in high regard. If we are ever going to be able to live out our professed values, we will have to get our schedules under control, which will mean denying ourselves and our kids some things we want. When our values and priorities have not been clearly articulated, the biggest fires, the most urgent demands get our time and energy.

4. Learn to accept trials as part of the human experience.

We have not been created to live stress-free lives. In fact, God made us to cope with the mental and biological effects of tremendous amounts of stress and trauma. We are naturally, by design, resilient people. God knew from the beginning that death and pain, heartaches and toothaches, would all be part of the human experience. In fact, Jesus promises that this life will include struggles: "In this world you will have trouble. But take heart! I have overcome the world" (John 16:33).

I'd like to see the first part of this verse on a coffee mug, but the promise that struggles will come isn't one we are quick to claim. In his second letter to the church at Corinth, the apostle Paul says that we often find ourselves persecuted, afflicted, struck down, and perplexed (2 Corinthians 4:8-9). Trials are actually part of the normal human experience, and the sooner we come to terms with this fact of life, the sooner we can stop agonizing over how hard life has been on us.

MY BUSY SCHEDULE BECOMES AN EXCUSE FOR NOT DOING MANY OF THE HARDER THINGS THAT I CLAIM TO HOLD IN HIGH REGARD.

---

5. Reset yourself often.

OK, so trials and tribulations are not to be considered unexpected, and we can indeed survive just about anything this world can throw at us. But we have to do it God's way. We need to learn to frequently reset our stress and anxiety levels back to baseline by hitting the reset button between stressors. We need minor, quick resets each hour, where we can push back from the desk or walk to the water cooler and bring ourselves back into the moment, out of our heads. We need at least an hour each day that is free from stressors, when we can reset our nervous systems from the accumulation of the day's stress by shooting some baskets with the kids or walking the dog around the neighborhood. We need a full day each week (Sabbath, anyone?) to re-charge and reset our brains and bodies back to a peaceful state.

Like many commands in the Old Testament, the Fourth Commandment – keep the Sabbath holy – came with severe consequences when it wasn't honored (Exodus 31:14). This was God's way of telling the people that He was serious about the Sabbath, and He wasn't prepared to take *no* for an answer. He didn't want to hear that we had a busy week coming up and needed to get ready, or a biology exam the next day. He didn't want to hear about how we would start taking a Sabbath when the kids were older or after the craziness of college comes to an end. He didn't *suggest* we take a Sabbath each week – he *commanded* it.

Before we get all legalistic about the Sabbath, we need to see how Jesus handled it. In the New Testament, in His beautifully gracious way, Jesus taught that the command to rest each week from our labor was actually intended to be for *our benefit*, not simply some arbitrary rule for God to use to control us (Mark 2:27). He knew that we would work ourselves to the bone without some guidelines, a boundary that would help us to establish a rhythm of hard work and intentional rest.

The question is this: Are we going to trust Him? Are we willing to set aside all the things we think we need to do in order to find rest each week? Our answer isn't a matter of "being a good Christian" or "having enough faith," but it just may determine how well we handle the life He has given us and how effective we are at the good works he has called each of us to do.

If you don't take a regular Sabbath, you're not alone. Research shows that Americans, both Christians and not, rarely allow themselves a weekly rest. A 2017 Barna study reported that only 14% of Americans intentionally set aside a day for rest each week, and less than 3% are actually successful at keeping that day completely work-free.[3] Is it any wonder that we are exhausted? I can only imagine how my family and spiritual life would be different if I was able to join the 3% consistently.

6. Set and keep clear boundaries.

We are finite and can't do it all, but didn't Jesus sacrifice everything to serve us? In the end He did, but we have to admit that His calling, His purpose was and is a bit different than ours. While Jesus spent His life loving and serving others, He also took care of himself. He would frequently retreat to the mountains, wilderness, or the lake to find some relief from the crowds and seek restoration by spending time with the Father. Even His teachings implied that we need to take care of ourselves: "Love your neighbor as yourself" (Mark 12:31).

The phrase "as yourself" implies that you love yourself. Now, this doesn't mean that you feel warm fuzzies about yourself, or that you are narcissistic or self-absorbed; it simply means that you take care of yourself and do what is best for you within limits. The implication is that we are unable to adequately love others without first loving ourselves. If you mistreat your heart, soul, mind, and body through neglect and abuse, how can you possibly love your neighbor in any healthy way? You and I cannot possibly give what we have not ourselves first received. Setting up boundaries, giving ourselves permission to say no to requests on our time and energy, is an important step in our ability to get our crazy busy lives under control again. Jesus did it and so can you.

A word of caution about boundaries. When life feels out of control, it is tempting to drop activities that will have the least immediate consequences, even when those are the very things that re-charge and reset us. When the kids' activities schedule fills the weekly calendar, it is easy to believe that you should stop going to the gym in the mornings, or playing Saturday afternoon basketball with the guys, or attending your Wednesday night Bible study at the church. Remember, we have to be strategic about what boundaries we set and what we say yes or no to. The activities that help reset your heart and mind and body are some of the most important things you do each week. Let them go at your own risk!

7. Discover why you are crazy busy.

Aside from accepting our human limits and intentionally and strategically setting up boundaries to protect margin in our schedules, for lasting change to occur it is critical that we dig deep and discover the *why* behind our crazy busy. If it is truly due to circumstances beyond our control, which is very uncommon, then accepting the things we cannot change may be the only option. If your overwhelming life is, like most, due to choices you have made, you need to figure out why you are allowing it to control you.

You may find it helpful to review the previous chapter as you consider your *why*. Is it a matter of pride or a need for affirmation?

Are you avoiding dealing with your hurts, hang-ups, and habits? Or are there simply too many good opportunities and you haven't yet learned to say no to the good so that you can say yes to the best? Whatever the underlying causes, until they are identified and challenged, any changes you make will be temporary. Lasting changes in behavior and feelings require lasting changes in the way we think.

It sometimes feels like the flow of our culture is running faster and faster each year, and we can so easily get swept up in the current without even realizing it. If life feels overwhelming or out of control, it may be time to step back and take an inventory of all you have on your plate. How did it all get there? Is everything on your calendar necessary for a fulfilling and God-honoring life? Where can you see opportunities to make positive changes that will bring back a sense of peace and joy along with some margin and rest in your life and the lives of those around you? Where can you create some breathing room in your schedule?

In the next chapter we will spend some time thinking about how our expectations – of life circumstances, other people, ourselves, and God – can lead to either a state of disappointment and frustration or one of peace and contentment. Very few thoughts can have a greater impact on our stress, anxiety, and depression.

7 Ways to Fight Back Against Crazy Busy

The frenetic pace of our modern lives is a major contributing factor to our stress, anxiety, and depression. But we don't actually have to live this way. It's not required. We can push back against crazy busy and reclaim our lives, and in the process, we can reclaim our sanity, peace, and joy. Here are a few places you can start:

1. Confess you are finite.

2. Build margin into your life.

3. Clarify your priorities.

4. Learn to accept trials as part of the human experiences.

5. Reset yourself often.

6. Set and keep clear boundaries.

7. Discover why you are crazy busy.

Download and print this list at
https://davidedwardcummings.com.

GREAT EXPECTATIONS

Disappointment with Our Circumstances, Ourselves, and the People around Us

"If you don't expect too much from me, you might not be let down."
The Gin Blossoms, *Hey Jealousy*[1]

I came home from work one early April evening, tired from a long day of teaching and an hour of my life lost sitting in traffic.

"Hi, Dad," a couple of the kids called out.

"Hi, honey. How was your day?" Ann asked without turning around from the stove, where she was parked, fixing something for dinner that smelled like baked chicken with garlic and parmesan.

As I set my backpack down, I noticed a white cardboard box on the kitchen counter that looked suspiciously like a donut box. My eyes got wider.

"Did you get donuts?" I asked with excitement.

I opened the box to find my absolute favorite donut: sometimes called a Bavarian, it's custard-filled with chocolate icing. My absolute favorite!

"We saved that one for you," Ann said with a warm tone of love in her voice.

She's so sweet.

She was still busy at the stove, and the kids were all running around setting the table and filling glasses with water. Had I not been distracted by the promise of the rich chocolate-and-custard goodness waiting for me, I might have thought that it was odd that no one in the room was looking at me. I gave Ann the customary three-count to tell me not to eat it before dinner (I may have counted a little faster than usual) and quickly got started.

I closed my eyes and wrapped my mouth around as much of the pastry as I could fit into it. This was exactly what the doctor ordered after a hard day. My brain was anticipating first the rich chocolate icing to be followed soon after by the light dough collapsing under my teeth. Only milliseconds later the crowning achievement of baking, the custard, would reach my taste buds, and I would slip into a temporary ecstasy, a sugar- and chocolate- and dough- and custard-induced escape from an exhausting Tuesday.

But something other than custard hit my taste buds. It was tangy, sweet and acrid like vinegar, but a little salty too. I stopped chewing and looked at the donut. The opening I had made was now dripping with a thick red substance. Ketchup. My sweet wife had bought my favorite kind of donut, painstakingly sucked out all of the custard with a turkey baster and replaced it with Heinz Ketchup. The final detail was a dab of custard over the hole where the ketchup had been added. It was the perfect April Fool's Day prank, and I was the perfect April Fool.

You have to understand, I usually like ketchup, especially on potatoes. If I had been taking a bite of salty fries that I had just dipped in ketchup, I wouldn't have reacted the way that I did. I would have savored it, in fact. But I wasn't expecting ketchup – I was expecting Bavarian custard. My brain was anticipating sweet and creamy, and I got tangy and saucy.

The result was that I almost gagged, and I had to spit it out in the kitchen sink. Ann and the kids busted out in laughter, finally turning around to see my face. They got me good. Of course, for the rest of the night I complained that there was no *actual* Bavarian donut waiting for me somewhere, to set things right again. I was left with the sensory memory of a chocolate and ketchup donut seared into my mind. A bit disappointing.

One of the most important lessons I have learned through my experiences with chronic stress and anxiety is that my expectations have the power to influence my interpretation of life, mental health, and spiritual well-being. As I reflected on the past several years with sober judgment, I realized that much of my inability to successfully cope with its challenges was due to a sense of disappointment in how it was all turning out. Reality wasn't lining up with my expectations. I was expecting custard, but I was getting ketchup.

Unmet expectations can cause disappointment, discouragement, and even dismay. We feel let down by ourselves, other people, and God. These disappointments can cause us to lose our focus and even lose our hope. This becomes particularly problematic when we dwell on them, replaying all the what-ifs and if-onlys in our minds over and over again. Until we identify and deal with our disappointments, we can get stuck, spinning our wheels but getting nowhere.

In the following sentence, fill in the blank with whatever you expected to be true of your life circumstances at this stage that hasn't come to pass: "I always thought by now _____ _____."

- I always thought by now *I would have gotten out of debt.*
- I always thought by now *I wouldn't still be living paycheck to paycheck.*
- I always thought by now *I would own a home rather than still be renting a place to live.*
- I always thought by now *I would be driving a nicer car, or at least a more reliable one.*
- I always thought by now *I would have saved enough to retire.*
- I always thought by now *I would be married.*
- I always thought by now *I would have children.*
- I always thought by now *I would have made management.*

- I always thought by now *I would be living someplace warmer.*
- I always thought by now *I would own my own business.*

For many of us, life hasn't turned out the way we had expected or hoped it would. We've had to face the harsh truth that some of our youthful dreams are simply never going to become reality, and the life we had hoped for is not the life we are living. Many of the things we had expected – not just hopes and dreams, but unquestioned expectations – are just not in the cards for us. If we're honest, most of us have to admit that we are a little disappointed in how things have turned out.

UNMET EXPECTATIONS CAN CAUSE DISAPPOINTMENT, DISCOURAGEMENT, AND EVEN DISMAY.

Some disappointments take the form of regrets, where unmet expectations meet guilt and cause us to wish we could go back in time and do things differently. Replaying old regret tapes in our heads prevents us from enjoying the blessings of today by perpetually pondering the what-could-have-beens of the past. They keep us stuck in the past, where nothing can be changed. The more we dwell on what didn't turn out the way we had hoped or expected, the less we can truly enjoy the present and all it has to offer us.

Many of my expectations of life, it turned out, were unfair, unrealistic, and unbiblical. For example, I had always assumed that I would be wealthy one day. I imagined living in a grand home with several acres of property, a couple of luxury cars in the driveway next to the boat and RV. I even pictured a second home someplace, maybe a cabin in the mountains or a beach house. We would vacation in the Bahamas and take weekend jaunts to Europe. In my mind, these weren't just dreams or wishes – for some reason, I actually *expected* that this would be my lifestyle as an adult!

Material expectations can be particularly dangerous. For one thing, available products differ from one generation to the next, making our expectations about our possessions entirely a matter of comparison. Tripp says, "Our desires for physical things morph into 'needs,' and when they do, we become completely convinced that we cannot live without them."[2]

Consider smartphones. A little over a decade ago, smartphones didn't even exist. No one felt that they needed mobile internet in their pockets, making it such a high priority as to displace actual necessities. Today, when I take a smartphone away from one of my teenagers as a consequence for some poor decision, they respond as if I have denied them food and water, or access to the bathroom. Practically overnight the smartphone has gone from a mere dream to a luxury to a God-given right and absolute necessity. Our view of this technology has changed in the blink of an eye, as have our expectations regarding it.

We are not doing ourselves any favors by embracing what my friend Dave Bruno calls "American-style consumerism" in his insightful book *The 100 Thing Challenge*.[3] Dave shows that even Christians, who have arguably more reason to be content than anyone else on Earth, have bought into the lie that more stuff will make us happy.

Financial guru Dave Ramsey used to have a huge billboard on Interstate 5 in Los Angeles that showed him pointing his finger at you as you drove by and a caption that read, "Act your wage!" It seems like such a simple principle: Spend less than you earn. Perfectly logical common sense, right? But how many of us are living paycheck to paycheck? How many times have I felt that I "need" or "deserve" or "should have" something in my life that the budget simply says I can't afford? Incidentally, many people try to solve this dilemma by inappropriately moving some of their wants and desires from their Cannot-Change List (maybe we need a separate Cannot-Afford List) to their Can-Change (Can-Afford) List by way of debt.

We are more indebted to creditors than ever before, and much of it is to support our unsupportable lifestyles. We can borrow money for everything from houses and cars to furniture and even appliances. We can borrow money to go to college or to go to Europe on vacation. I saw a commercial just yesterday that offered financing for a teeth-whitening service! Far too often, we don't act our wage, to use Dave Ramsey's phrase. Our discontentment causes us to overextend our budgets and live beyond our means, but our stuff doesn't bring any lasting satisfaction. Bruno says, "The trouble is that no store keeps ultimate contentment in its inventory."[3]

The average American is deeply indebted to various creditors and will likely remain in debt until the day he or she dies. One study reported that 65% of American adults are under so much financial pressure that it causes them to lose sleep at night.[4] More than half of American families have had to make significant sacrifices (*e.g.*, taking on a second job or new credit card debt) in order to pay their rent or mortgage.[5] Among households with credit card debt, the average balance is nearly $17,000 per family, amounting to almost $1,300 in interest payments alone each year.[6] Student loan debts average over $50,000 per student, and we owe about $30,000 per vehicle that we have financed.[6]

Debt and depression frequently go hand in hand, but it is not always clear which is the cause and which is the effect.[7] It is likely that they feed off of one another, the stress of debt causing depression, and the fog of depression leading to poor spending choices that exacerbate debt in a vicious cycle.

Every so often I travel to Latin America for ministry or work. When I do, I am honored to visit the homes of local people, who may not have much by American standards, but are more than happy to share what they do have with a visitor. I always return from these trips convicted of my own material greed and inspired to seek a new level of contentment with my own home and personal possessions. Seeing how little others have puts my own circumstances into perspective. Sadly, not long after returning home, my perspective easily switches back to that of an American used to having lots of nice things, and my old friend discontentment creeps back in.

Where does this discontentment come from? The first and arguably most important source of discontentment is our own hearts. The Bible calls us greedy and selfish, and that's on our good days. We envy one another rather than rejoicing in the different ways God has blessed each of us. We covet what was not given to us and resent the one to whom it was given. Like school children, we demand that

God be "fair" and give us the same good things He has given to others. With an air of entitlement, we cross our arms and pout and threaten to hold our breath until our demands are met.

The culture around us certainly does not help our discontentment – if anything, it encourages it. A recent car ad claimed, "It's not more than you need, just more than you're used to." The entire M.O. of advertising is to convince you that you want, need, deserve more than what you have.

- Already have a nice car? This one's better.
- Your hair can be prettier with this product.
- Your clothes are so last year.
- You'll be less socially awkward if you drink this beer.

Bruno writes, "dissatisfaction is implicit in the fabric of consumerism."[3] If we all learned to be content, where would capitalism be? Capitalism requires that the majority of us be deeply discontent.

Our homes, no longer places for safety and hospitality, have become the latest fashion trends, costing us a fortune to update and remodel every few years just to stay current. It's bad enough when we're discarding a perfectly good pair of jeans just because they are no longer the latest fashion. But maybe we've gone too far when we begin gutting and remodeling a $50,000 kitchen just because it is outdated. The culture around us stirs up the natural discontentment and envy in our hearts and convinces us that we need whatever the latest thing is. The result is that we never allow ourselves to be fully content.

In a 2015 survey by the American Psychological Association, 64% of respondents cited financial concerns as a primary source of stress, more common than any other source including work, the economy, family responsibilities, and personal health.[8] In 2017, the APA reported that personal finances were the #2 stressor in our lives, second only to "the future of our nation," with 62% of the participants reporting that "money" was their primary stressor.[9]

Financial stress is clearly a major burden on the minds and hearts of Americans, and I was no different. How much of my financial struggle was based on legitimate problems, and how much was due to my twisted expectations? I didn't want to face the truth, that God had indeed provided more than enough for my family to be safe and secure and to have a reasonably happy life if I would just live within my means.

Discontentment is a joy-killer. In fact, it's just a plain old killer. Few things can drain all of our peace, joy, happiness, grace, mercy, hope, generosity, or hospitality more than a discontented heart. King Solomon observed that envy – a form of discontentment aimed at others – can destroy us (Proverbs 14:30), and the apostle Paul warned that discontentment with money will "plunge people into ruin and destruction" (1 Timothy 6:9).

Probably the most thorough passage on contentment in Scripture is found in chapter 6 of the gospel of Matthew.

Do not store up for yourselves treasures on earth, where moths and vermin destroy, and where thieves break in and steal. But store up for yourselves treasures in heaven, where moths and vermin do not destroy, and where thieves do not break in and steal. For where your treasure is, there your heart will be also. (Matthew 6:19-21)

Jesus very clearly distinguishes the temporary nature of treasures on earth from the eternal nature of treasures in heaven. "Treasures on earth" refers to anything that is not permanent. My house, my laptop, my fly fishing rods, and my bank account are all temporary luxuries. Some day they will be gone and no one will even remember them, including me. "Treasures in heaven," on the other hand, refers to anything eternal, and as my wise friend Doug taught me when I was a new Christian, there are only two things eternal in this world: God and the souls of people. According to Jesus, these are the things most worthy of investing my life in because the things I treasure most are the things that will lead my heart. This is what Jesus meant when He told the Pharisee that the greatest commandment in all of Scripture is to love God with everything you have, and that the second greatest is like it – to love your neighbor as yourself (Matthew 22:36-39). God and people – these are His top priorities, and He wants them to be ours, as well.

Besides, He tells His disciples, all this worrying about temporary things will get you nowhere.

So do not worry, saying "What shall we eat?" or "What shall we drink?" or "What shall we wear for clothing?" For the pagans run after all these things, and your heavenly Father knows that you need them. But seek first His kingdom and His righteousness, and all these things will be given to you as well. (Matthew 6:31-33)

Do you hear what Jesus is saying? He's telling us that we don't have to live in fear for the basic necessities of life. God knows exactly what we need, and we can trust Him to meet those needs. Our focus, instead, should be on the righteousness and kingdom of God. If you made a to-do list for today, grab a pen and write in big letters across the top

#1 SEEK HIS KINGDOM AND HIS RIGHTEOUSNESS.

Everything else on the list you can stop worrying about.

I want to be sure that I am clear about something. The passage in Matthew 6 is not promising to give you all of the things you *want* in life or that life is always going to be easy. It's also not saying that it's OK for you to quit your job and stop providing for your family and paying the bills because God is going to do that for you. Generally speaking, *you* are God's plan for providing those things. Although it is God who gives you the ability to produce wealth (Deuteronomy 8:18), *you* must still wake up in the morning and go to work to earn it. Matthew 6 is not a call to stop taking care of business. Instead it is a call to stop *worrying* about taking care of business and to focus your mental and emotional energies on eternal things like your relationship with God and other people.

To cover short-term expenses when we first moved to San Diego, Ann and I were looking for opportunities to sell off anything we didn't absolutely need at the moment. I dug out my old hockey gear from the garage and sold it on Craigslist. As our youngest, outgrew any of his clothes, we were quick to find a way to cash them in just in time to buy the next sizes up for everyone.

One item I was eager to sell was Ann's mountain bike. We had bought it during graduate school for $350, a huge sum of money considering how little we had to live on. Ann got pregnant just a few months later, so the bike didn't get much use. In fact, by the time we were living in California again, the bike couldn't have had more than 50 miles on it; the tires still had the original little whiskers leftover from when the rubber was poured into the mold. This was essentially a brand new bike, so it should be worth something, right?

I posted the bike for sale on the internal classified ads at the University. The posting read like this:

Raleigh M80 Mountain Bike for Sale
Like New – Barely Used – Fewer Than 50 Miles
Paid $350, Asking $150

When a young woman from one of the administrative departments emailed me saying she was interested, I worked up my courage to ask Ann to bring it out to campus so she could see it. You have to understand that Ann was at home with three young kids, all under the age of five. Getting through the day was difficult enough without having to try to get all three of them napped, fed, dressed and into the van for an hour-long drive in heavy traffic. And there was that thing about getting the bike into the van somehow, but Ann saw the value in it so she graciously agreed to bring it out to campus that afternoon.

I stood in a parking lot talking with the prospective buyer when our silver Dodge Grand Caravan pulled up. When Ann opened the driver's side door, I could hear more than one child crying. *Uh oh.* As Ann stepped out of the van, she shot me a look that said, "someone is going to pay for this." I quickly pulled the bike out of the van so the young lady could take it for a test drive around campus while Ann and I tried to keep the kids occupied on a nearby strip of grass next to the parking lot. Apparently, naps were all out of whack and everyone was getting hungry, so the kids weren't too happy. It had been a tough couple of hours for all four of them.

When the woman returned from her jaunt around campus, she excitedly told us that she really liked the bike and it was exactly what she was looking for.

"I'll give you $10 for it."

I felt my posture sink with disappointment as her words hit my ears. I only hoped Ann didn't hear her make that ridiculous offer.

"You do realize that we're asking $150 for this bike, right?" I responded, trying to keep my composure.

"Yeah," she replied. "But $10 is what I'm willing to spend right now."

At this point I think I had the "someone's going to pay for this" look on my face, so I just bit my tongue and calmly loaded the bike back into the van. After helping Ann get the kids strapped into their car seats, I gave her a cautious kiss on the cheek, apologized for wasting her afternoon, and said I'd be home shortly behind them. This was not how I had expected the day to go.

People from all walks of life let us down: family, strangers, co-workers. Everyone. Everyone has the potential to frustrate, disappoint, anger, and exasperate us. The key that controls how we react to others is what we expect of them in the first place.

Your nuclear family, also known as the conjugal family, is not the family we were born or adopted into, but instead is the family we have chosen and created through marriage and childbirth or adoption. These are arguably the most important relationships in our lives. We spend more time with these people than with anyone else, and we are more invested in these relationships than any others. If there was ever a place and a group of people who needed and deserved to know clearly what we expected from them, it is in our homes. Sadly, however, we often just assume that we are all on the same page or that our expectations are obvious without ever taking the time to articulate them. The result can be friction and dysfunction, simply because expectations weren't verbalized or consistent. Unexplored and unspoken expectations are a primary way we can get into trouble in our relationships.

In a marriage, it is important to know your own expectations, articulate them clearly to your spouse, and discuss them often. Are they reasonable and biblical expectations? How flexible are you willing to be? Do you know what your spouse expects from you, and are you willing and able to meet those expectations?

When you set expectations for your child, have you clearly and consistently articulated them? Have you empowered the child to meet those expectations? Are you being reasonable about the timeline in which you expect your child to be able to meet those expectations? If you have major goals for your kids that you want met by this weekend, you may be in for some real frustration – on both sides!

What about your friendships? What sort of expectations do you have of your friends, and are they reasonable? Do you expect them to put in as much effort as you do, or to make the friendship as much of a priority as you make it? If you are frustrated with or disappointed in one of your friends, you may need to carefully evaluate what you expect from them.

As we discussed in Chapter 6, the choices of other people are on the Cannot-Change List. I may have hopes for how someone I care about will respond to a challenge in our relationship, but I cannot control or change them in any way. Their thoughts, feelings, words, and behaviors are all beyond me. When they choose to respond in a way that hurts me, my only healthy course of action is to learn to accept it, with grace and serenity, giving it over to the Lord.

We can get quite uptight over the independent choices of any sovereign human being, be it a spouse, child, co-worker, friend, or complete stranger. If we have rigid expectations about how someone "should" or "should not" think, feel, or behave, we are setting ourselves up for serious disappointment, and possibly even conflict. Why? Because people have free will, sin is real, and our expectations are not always the law of the land.

One of the most unrealistic expectations we can have about others is that they will not make choices that will hurt us, but that's exactly what we should expect in a world where sin is not yet eliminated. Jesus came and died on the cross to save us from the penalty of our sins, but until we are free of this "perishable" body (1 Corinthians

15:42), the war will rage on between our sinful nature and our new nature in Christ. Sanctification, the process of shedding our sin and becoming righteous like Christ, is a process that begins at salvation but is not completed until heaven. Sin is inevitable. Expecting others to never hurt us is like doing the dishes and expecting that you'll never have to wash them again.

How should we view the sins of others? First, we must stop expecting people to be perfect because that is not fair to them or to their personal sanctification journey. We are all works in progress. Second, we have to put the sins of others on the correct list, the Cannot-Change List. Your spouse will sin and hurt you. Your kids will sin and hurt you. Your parents, siblings, friends, co-workers, neighbors, and strangers will sin and hurt you. Expecting anything different, or expecting that somehow you can prevent it from happening, will only cause you heartache and disappointment. Finally, we must learn to forgive.

WE MUST STOP EXPECTING PEOPLE TO BE PERFECT BECAUSE THAT IS NOT FAIR TO THEM.

Dr. Fred Luskin directs the Stanford University Forgiveness Project, a psychology research program aimed at understanding the mental and biological impacts of both holding and forgiving grudges.[10] Luskin says that a grievance (a grudge or an unforgiveness) is formed in our minds when we perceive that someone has hurt us, we blame them for the pain and trouble it causes, and we create a narrative in our minds around the hurt. Luskin says that forgiveness involves learning to take the offense less personally, blaming the person less for what they did and changing the narrative from a grievance story (where you are the victim) to a forgiveness story (where you are the hero).

In his book *Forgive for Good*, Luskin describes research into the psychological and physical effects of forgiveness.[10] Holding a grudge, according to the research, does substantial damage to our minds and bodies. Unforgiveness increases stress, which in turn can cause or aggravate anxiety and depression. Depression is a risk factor for both heart disease and stroke, while increased stress causes muscle tension and general physical feelings of discomfort. An unwillingness to forgive increases feelings of anger and hostility, which in turn decrease cardiovascular function and increase blood pressure, and reduce heart rate variability, which is essential for healthy heart function, all conspiring to raise the risk of heart disease.

Forgiveness, on the other hand, comes with abundant mental and physical benefits. Stress, and associated anxiety and depression, are relieved with forgiveness. Forgiveness reduces muscle tension and results in fewer medically diagnosed chronic conditions. Blood pressure and heart rate come down, and heart variability increases. Feelings of anger and hostility are lessened and overall cardiovascular function improves. Forgiveness leads to more positive emotions including optimism and hope, compassion for others, less anger, and greater self-confidence. Notably, people who forgive reported fewer physical symptoms of stress and anxiety, including dizziness, stomachaches, headaches, muscle aches, and fatigue, the effects of which persisted at least several months after forgiveness training. The research showed that forgiveness is really good for us mentally and physically. Who knew?

UNFORGIVENESS INCREASES STRESS, WHICH IN TURN CAN CAUSE OR AGGRAVATE ANXIETY AND DEPRESSION.

Not surprisingly, the Bible has much to say about forgiveness. In God's economy, forgiveness is a requirement, not a suggestion. It is not some spontaneous emotion you feel as if the other person's words and actions don't hurt anymore, nor is it something you wait to come upon you like the desire to eat or sleep. It is a conscious choice to let it go and move on rather than holding it over or against them. In Wm. Paul Young's bestseller *The Shack*, Papa, representing God, put it this way to Mack, who lost his daughter to a serial killer: "Forgiveness is not about forgetting, Mack. It is about letting go of another person's throat."[11]

In fact, the Bible says that unless you willingly choose to forgive others the sins they have committed that have hurt you, God will not forgive you of your sins. That's a scary thought. Listen to the words of Jesus after teaching His disciples the Lord's Prayer:

"For if you forgive other people when they sin against you, your heavenly Father will also forgive you. But if you do not forgive others their sins, your Father will not forgive your sins." (Matthew 6:14-15)

Besides fearing God's judgment, what is to be our motivation for offering forgiveness? Forgiveness of others, according to Scripture, is the appropriate response to the forgiveness we have received from God through the death and resurrection of Jesus. The apostle Paul wrote, "Be kind and compassionate to one another, forgiving each other, just as in Christ God forgave you" (Ephesians 4:32). Understanding the forgiveness God has made available to us in Jesus Christ is essential to our ability to forgive others and thereby receive His forgiveness. If you don't understand how much you have been forgiven, both past and present, you are not going to be a particularly forgiving person. The Amish have a proverb that might be worth committing to memory: "We can stop forgiving others when Christ stops forgiving us."[12]

Each of us is a slave to sin, and we should expect nothing less than selfishness and spite where sin is concerned. However, it may be that the person who we feel has let us down is simply exercising his or her right to make the choices they feel are best. In the first case, where sin is clearly involved, we need to learn to be forgiving people. In the second case, where sin is not a part of the equation, we must ask ourselves whether we have the right to place those particular expectations on someone else. Until we learn to have realistic, reasonable, and biblical expectations of others, we will be setting ourselves up for pain and disappointment.

Do you remember the "I always thought by now" experiment we tried earlier in the chapter? We were considering ways that we were disappointed with how life was turning out for us. Now it's time to run the same mental experiment, but this time focusing on ourselves. How would you finish the statement "I always thought by now ____ _____," but with regard to who you are becoming as a human being?

- I always thought by now *I would have gone back to school to earn a degree.*
- I always thought by now *I would be in a career that I enjoyed, something that had some significance.*
- I always thought by now *I would have lost those extra pounds.*
- I always thought by now *I would have my diabetes under control.*
- I always thought by now *I would be free from anxiety and depression.*
- I always thought by now *I would feel closer to God.*
- I always thought by now *I would a better leader at home.*
- I always thought by now *I would have conquered that specific sin in my life.*

So often we are harder on ourselves than we are on anyone else. It can be much easier to offer grace to other people than it is to tolerate disappointment, frustration, and unmet expectations in ourselves. It's as if we think we should be above problems and struggles, as if we should not be bound by time and space limits, as if those things are for other people, not us.

As we grow older, the opportunity to reach some goals and dreams fades. Where once we had something to look forward to – college, career, family – we have now "arrived" and wonder what's next. We may experience questions, doubts, and even regrets about things like our choice of a career or spouse, and the way we raised our children.

AS LONG AS WE ALLOW THE WORLD TO DEFINE US, WE WILL ALWAYS STRUGGLE WITH DISAPPOINTMENT IN OURSELVES.

As I quietly slipped into my forties, many of these disappointments and regrets began to surface in my mind. I wasn't convinced that I was becoming the man God intended me to become, the man I had expected to become. Where had I gone wrong? How was it that I was still battling some of the very same struggles from my youth, even from my BC (before Christ) days? Frustration and disappointment due to unmet self-expectations were dragging me down. I worked harder and tried to avoid too much self-reflection. I took on more at work and church, hoping that by sheer busyness I could get on track. All I managed to do, however, was suppress the inner conflicts and turmoil, letting them ferment into a stinky, acidic soup of pain and confusion.

At the heart of much of our self-disappointment lies the following question: From where, or from whom, do we derive our meaning, purpose, and identity in this life? If we allow the world to define us, then we are nothing more than a job, a consumer, and a taxpayer. These definitions fall terribly short of who we truly are. Maybe we think we're getting closer when we see ourselves as a parent, a child, a sibling, or a spouse. While these are all important roles in life, they are not guaranteed to be permanent and form a shaky foundation for building an identity.

Even roles and responsibilities that are tied in with ministry – pastor, missionary, elder – are a far cry from the radiant, beautiful soul the Lord made us to be: we are children of the Creator of the universe! We are loved, wanted, and even needed. We were bought at an incomparably high price, and now we belong to the One who purchased us, not to be slaves again, but to be free, as we were meant to be. As long as we allow the world to define us, we will always struggle with disappointment in ourselves, in others, in our life circumstances, and in God Himself.

Having expectations is a normal part of life, but we need to be mindful in order to know and understand them better. We need to test them against the is-it-fair-reasonable-and-biblical standard. In many cases, our life circumstances are beyond our control. Some circumstances can be courageously changed, but others must be serenely accepted in order to find peace. When we are disappointed or frustrated with other people, if it is a matter of sin on their part, forgiveness is God's solution. When the other person is not in sin, we need to allow them to make the decisions they think are best without judgment or condemnation. Finally, disappointment with ourselves requires grace – accepting God's grace freely offered to us on the cross, and offering and accepting grace to ourselves. We are often so much harder on ourselves than we are on the people we love. We need to learn to offer that same grace, compassion, and mercy to ourselves that we so readily extend to our loved ones. Unmet expectations can completely derail our happiness, but it is within our power to examine them and set new expectations, expectations that fair and reasonable and biblical sound. We can indeed overcome this insidious source of stress, anxiety, and depression.

THE RESILIENCE WORKSHOP PART I

Psychological Strategies for Coping with and Building Resilience to Stress, Anxiety, and Depression

"Do not conform to the pattern of this world, but be transformed by the renewing of your mind."
Romans 12:2a

For the past decade I have been teaching an ecology class in Costa Rica every year or two. Some years I bring a group of students from my university for a couple weeks of traipsing around the cloud and rain forests, experiencing the ecosystems we have been studying in the classroom. Other years I support the classes another college is holding in Costa Rica by flying down and teaching a module in person. On one such trip to teach students from another university, I started having panic attacks – the first setback since recovering from my breakdown a few years before.

I didn't have a clue what caused it. I don't like flying, so I'm sure the long trip with multiple flights didn't help. I usually travel with my own students or bring members of my family, but on this trip I didn't know a single soul. I felt like I had so much work to get done back home that I didn't have the time to spare for this trip. Just to add to the situation, I was attacked by a migraine on the drive into the remote cloud forest station where I'd be housed for the next ten days. If you've never had a migraine, you need to know that it is so much more than just a bad headache. My vision was warped due to what doctors call an aura, a moving, growing patch of diffracted light that impairs my ability to see anything. I was nauseous, a sensation not helped by the windy, narrow Pan-American Highway. Oh, and my head felt like someone had just hit me in the temple with a baseball bat. OK, maybe I did have a clue what caused it after all.

The first sense of panic hit me as we descended from the crest of the mountain range down into the valley. I've been there many times before, and all of my memories from this place are positive. The beauty of a tropical cloud forest is unlike anything else on the planet, but my response was a racing heart, sweaty hands, and a tingling sensation all over my body as if I was hiding under a counter and a velociraptor was hunting for me (remember that terrifying scene in Jurassic Park?). Tingling isn't the right word – more like a burning sensation, like fire running through my veins, making me want to crawl out of my own skin. All I wanted to do was jump out of the truck and start running. It made no sense.

At the field station, I met the students I'd be teaching for the next week and sat down for supper with them. They were all excited to have a visitor and eager to talk. I wanted to run away – or cry. I didn't understand what was happening to me, why I felt so overwhelmed with fear by something that was familiar and good and exciting. I excused myself early for bed, making the excuse that I was exhausted from the last two days of traveling. In my room, I broke down. The more I thought about the fact that I was having a panic attack, the first in almost four years, the more panicky I became. *What if I can't get this under control? What if I have to be hospitalized here in Costa Rica? What is everyone going to think of me if I can't do my job? What's wrong with me that I'm turning an amazing trip into a nightmare of fear?*

The next day was Pascua, Easter Sunday. I had been really looking forward to attending Easter mass with the local Ticos, but now I was dreading facing anyone. I went for a walk by myself, but I couldn't shake the feeling of dread. I just wanted to be back at home, but I still had another week here, and thinking about that just got me more riled up. I had to do something, but what?

I talked to my wife that day and confessed to her that I was having a hard time with my anxiety. Just seeing her on FaceTime was a boost. I also got to talk to the kids and even "played" with the dog. But once I hung up the phone, the anxiety rose up again like a tea kettle on the stove about to boil over into panic. This wasn't subsiding. I had to do something.

I mustered up the courage to go downstairs and ask the station managers for a private conversation. I told them my history with anxiety and explained that I was feeling overwhelmed and unsure of how to proceed. After a long, compassionate conversation, we decided it was best for me to head back home. There, at least, I could see my therapist, and maybe just being back with my family, in familiar surroundings, I could reset myself and start the hard work of trying to unpack this experience, to figure out what went wrong.

Packing up my gear and heading back to the airport felt like such a defeat. I really thought I had my anxiety better under control. I thought I could handle traveling again. *I should be able to handle this. I shouldn't have to turn tail and go home again.* At the same time, once we made the decision to head back home, I could physically feel a change in my body. With every mile we drove closer to the airport, I grew more relaxed. I didn't enjoy the flight home, but boy was it good to see my wife at the airport when I landed. Over the next couple of weeks, my mind and body slowly reset back down to baseline levels, and my therapist and I began unpacking what had happened.

The take-home point of this story is that we can all find ourselves in a bad place and in need of tools to help us face the situation. Even when we think we have our struggles under control, we should be prepared for the occasional setback. Coping skills don't come naturally for most of us, but must be learned and practiced in order to become useful. Even more important than coping skills for dealing with life as it happens, we can build long-term resilience to stress, anxiety, and depression so that when they do hit us we're not overpowered by them.

Let me confess that I do not have this whole thing figured out – like you, I am still on a journey toward wholeness. What I have learned, though, I will gladly share with you. In the next two chapters I will briefly describe some of the most powerful coping skills available to you. Many of these strategies, when practiced regularly, have been shown to build resilience. Some will sound weird and may not be a good fit for your personality. Your job is to find a couple of them that you can relate to and begin learning all you can about them, how they work, and how to implement them. And then practice, practice, practice. If you're seeing a therapist or pastoral counselor, I would recommend that you bring these two chapters with you to one of your sessions and discuss your options with a trained professional.

EVEN WHEN WE THINK WE HAVE OUR STRUGGLES UNDER CONTROL, WE SHOULD BE PREPARED FOR THE OCCASIONAL SETBACK.

Over the past few years I have read countless books, talked with therapists, and listened to innumerable friends, pastors, and complete strangers about coping skills that work the best. As you can probably imagine, people and situations are all so very different from one another that there is no single magic bullet that works for everyone. In this first "resilience workshop" we will focus our attention on *psychological strategies* for coping with and building resilience to stress, anxiety, and depression. Then, in the following chapter we will turn our attention to *physical, social, and spiritual approaches*. My hope and prayer is that some of these tools will be as helpful to you as they have been to me.

The American Psychological Association defines resilience as "the process of adapting well in the face of adversity, trauma, tragedy, threats or significant sources of stress – such as family and relationship problems, serious health problems or workplace and financial stressors."[1] Others call upon the discipline of physics to define resilience as "the capability of an object to resume its original size and shape after deformation."[2] Who wouldn't want resilience!

Ultimately, this is the goal of all of our coping strategies, rather than simply surviving the moment. There will always be challenges, stressors, traumas, and tragedies to cope with. There will always be bears on the loose. Building resilience means learning how to bounce back after you've come face to face with one of those hairy beasts, and, better yet, how to keep the bears out of your camp in the first place.

1. Talk to a counselor.

I am a big fan of getting a set of professional eyes and ears on your situation when you're struggling. Talking with an objective counselor can be one of the most beneficial tools in your toolkit. There is absolutely nothing you can say that will shock your therapist! A therapist can be like a guide on a trail that you've never been down before. She can help you stay on the path and find your way out of the forest without getting lost. She can give you confidence that you're not the first person to go down this trail and that you can and will find your way out again. My therapists have always been cheerleaders, inspiring me onward to the victory and helping me to believe in myself. They've also been a set of clear eyes who are able to see what's going on when I am too close to the situation to see it for myself.

If you are avoiding seeing a therapist, it may be that you don't trust them, and you don't have faith that what they do can actually help anyone. Some people call psychology a "soft science," but reality is that psychology is a very old science based on thousands of years of close and careful observations of human beings. It's true that the brain is vastly more complicated than any other structure in all of the biological world. It's also true that it's very difficult to run laboratory experiments on live human brains (something about ethics...). That does not mean, however, that the psychology community has not made great strides in understanding the mind, and it certainly does not mean that a therapist is unable to help you with your personal challenges.

Another objection I commonly hear is that Christians shouldn't need a therapist – we have Jesus! Yes, praise God that we have the Father who made us, the Son who saves us, and the Spirit who guides us. And yes, Scripture has much to say about stress, anxiety, and depression. If this is your philosophy, then it would also stand to reason that we don't need to see a lawyer when we get into legal trouble, or an accountant to help do our taxes, or an optometrist to prescribe a pair of reading glasses. According to this line of thinking, we also don't need a doctor when we have an infection or cancer. My opinion is that specialists are a gift from God, an extension of His grace to us. They are not perfect – they are human, but they have valuable expertise and much to offer to a hurting world. How much more of a blessing could you be to your family and friends, how much more of a witness for Christ could you be to your co-workers and neighbors if you were healthy and whole? Don't let unbiblical biases keep you from being all that God intends for you to be. In fact, many churches maintain lists of therapists who understand the faith component of your situation.

Even if you are not philosophically opposed to seeing a therapist, it's easy to procrastinate with any of a number of excuses:

- I don't have time for therapy sessions.
- I don't want to be perceived as weak or needy.
- I don't want _____ to find out.
- I don't want to be labeled.
- I can't afford it.
- I don't know of any good therapists.
- I'll get to it when _____.
- That might help other people, but I'm different.
- Therapists just spout a bunch of psychobabble that doesn't apply to real life.
- I tried that once and it didn't work.

Look into one-on-one talk therapy, group therapy, or a support group. If you don't know where to start, talk to your general practitioner for recommendations. If you are tech savvy, check out the internet. Almost every major city has free or low-cost care available; it may be a social worker rather than a psychiatrist who can prescribe medications, but it is a starting point for exploring therapy options. It may be a support group for people who have had similar experiences as you. For any excuse you may have, there is a way around it if you are willing.

2. Check your self-talk.

A big part of talk therapy is revealing and challenging thoughts that aren't accurate or are unhelpful. No one has more influence over our lives than we do, because no one talks to us as much as we talk to ourselves. We often tell ourselves inaccurate things – outright lies or half-truths that keep us stuck. Sometimes we tell ourselves the truth but in unhelpful, mean-spirited ways. We need to learn to recognize those inaccurate or unhelpful voices in our heads and challenge them with true and helpful statements. This takes time and practice, but it is very important if we are to find freedom from our mental and emotional struggles. This isn't about positive-thinking your way out of depression or anxiety. No, this is all about *accurate* thinking – a radical commitment to the truth, no matter the cost. Don't ignore ugly truths, but don't dwell on them, either. Accept and assign responsibility accurately. See crises realistically – not through rose-colored glasses, but also not as insurmountable obstacles.

Our brains have a natural negativity bias, meaning that they give more weight to negative thoughts than to positive ones. This makes sense if we're trying to survive in a harsh and dangerous world: it's more important to remember to never ever *ever* try to pet a lion cub than it is to remember how beautiful a sunset can be. In modern times, when survival is not typically dependent on us remembering and dwelling on the threats we might face, this negativity bias only drags us down, forming hurtful automatic thoughts and keeping us in crisis mode. You have the power to push back against automatic negativity, ruminating on negative thoughts, over-reacting to threats, and predicting catastrophic outcomes by challenging the way you think.

It can be easy, almost unconscious, for us to spin ourselves up in the midst of a challenge by telling ourselves outright lies or half-truths, or by focusing on unhelpful truths. Maybe you and your spouse are having a spat. Does it help for you to ruminate on everything you did or said that was hurtful? Is it really, honestly, entirely her fault, and are you really, honestly, completely innocent in this situation?

It's important to be aware of your self-talk, the inner monologue you have running, especially during a struggle. If you don't pay close attention to what you are saying to yourself, you will likely make matters worse. Ask yourself, Is this true? Is this helpful? A good test to see if your self-talk is helpful is to ask if you would be saying these same things to a close friend in the same situation. What can you do if you find that your self-talk is untrue or unhelpful? Challenge it with the truth and replace your condemning, harsh words with words you would use with a friend. Remember, what you say to yourself can make a tremendous difference in how you handle a stressor.

The late Bernard Meltzer is often credited as saying, "Before you speak ask yourself if what you are going to say is true, is kind, is necessary, is helpful. If the answer is no, maybe what you are about to say should be left unsaid."[3] We could all benefit from applying this advice to our self-talk.

Maybe we learned ineffective or shame-based coping strategies from our role models: Suck it up. Tough it out. Push through. Just get over it. Maybe we haven't been completely honest with ourselves and we've bought into hurtful lies about ourselves and others. Or maybe we've just adopted an overall negativity that is holding us back. Wherever we're off-track in our thinking, we can get back on track and find recovery and resilience by challenging the self-condemning lies with self-grace and truth.

3. Remind yourself of the truth about your situation.

First, remember that the deep lows don't last forever. The deep lows, the stuck times, can feel overwhelming. Remind yourself, right then and there, that life isn't always going to be like this, and that relief will come. Push back against despair. Remind yourself that in Christ you are not crushed, hopeless, destroyed, or abandoned (2 Corinthians 4:8-9), even when it feels like you are.

133

Second, remember that <u>how you are feeling is normal for someone struggling with anxiety or depression</u>. You are not the first person on earth to feel this way, nor are you the toughest, most inexplicable case in human history. Give yourself some grace and don't guilt yourself just because you are struggling. What you are experiencing is not pleasant, but it is not uncommon either. You are in good company.

Third, remember that <u>your judgment cannot be trusted when you are in the heat of the battle</u>. Your intense emotions are very real, but your decision-making processes and ability to judge your situation are impaired by neurochemicals like cortisol. This is not the time to buy a new car, quit your job, leave your husband, or get a tattoo. Don't make big decisions right now, and don't set enormous goals in the moment. When you are trying to process the words your wife just said about leaving you and the kids for another man, this is not the best time to decide that you are going to lose fifty pounds in the next six months or that you are finally going to start reading the Bible every single day (when you haven't picked it up once in the last year). Setting unrealistically grandiose goals only sets you up for more failure and disappointment, which you really don't need right now. Remember, your thoughts often lie to you, especially in the darkest hours. Don't trust everything you think, especially when you are down. If you're not sure, share your thoughts with someone you trust to see if you are thinking clearly.

4. Ground yourself in reality.

Grounding yourself means getting out of your head, snapping out of the world of mental words and abstract ideas, and anchoring yourself in reality. Don't lose yourself in the TV, computer, or phone. These escapes are OK in short doses, but hiding in them only delays healing and progress and can actually make matters worse. If you are having a tough time getting out of your head, lost in repetitive thoughts that are unhelpful, try focusing on your five senses: what do I see, smell, feel, hear, or taste right now? Be present in the moment in every way possible. When the intrusive thoughts press back in, calmly return your attention to the present moment. When the physical reality around you is not life-threatening, focusing on it can help you lower your stress level back to normal. When coupled with deep, slow breathing this practice of grounding yourself in the senses can be a powerful sedative.

This practice, often called mindfulness, is becoming a popular strategy among therapists for helping us to get out of our heads and into the real world. We need something to snap us out of it when we are stuck replaying the same self-talk tape in our minds, or telling ourselves the same inaccurate or unhelpful things about ourselves and our situation. Learning the practice of mindfulness, returning to the moment, to the sensory information from our eyes, ears, nose, mouth, and skin, can be just what is needed to break the cycle of stewing and ruminating on unhelpful thoughts. Besides, nothing else in life exists outside of the present moment, so why not live in it? Slow down and focus on one thing at a time, being fully present with that one thing and learning to ignore all the other things demanding your attention.

When we're lost in our own heads thinking about the past – conversations that were uncomfortable, regrets, or even the good old days – we increase our risk of depression or worsen depression that may already exist. Conversely, constantly thinking about what's yet to come, even if it's with excited anticipation, makes us more prone to anxiety. No matter what we're lost in thought about, we miss what's going on in the moment, and what's happening in the moment matters. Whether you are sitting in the bleachers at your kid's baseball game, or you're grieving the loss of your favorite pet, learning to be present in the moment, accepting the good feelings with the bad, is an important part of building resilience.

5. Accept the things you cannot change.

Acceptance is one of the most important short-term and long-term strategies for facing life's trials. Remember that how you perceive a stressor dictates how you will respond to it. If you can learn to accept disappointment, frustration, physical or emotional pain, loss, grief, failure, and other challenges, you can positively impact how you respond to these things. Understand that I'm not saying that you should quit trying to make your situation better, or that you should just give up hope for your circumstances to ever improve. But negative experiences are a fact of life, and the sooner we come to accept them as such, the sooner we can stop overreacting to them and find a path forward.

10 PSYCHOLOGICAL STRATEGIES FOR BUILDING RESILIENCE

There are numerous well-vetted techniques for overcoming stress, anxiety, and depression available in published books. Some are intended to help you in the moment when an emergency strikes. Others are best for building resilience to life's challenges over the long haul. Most are very helpful for both. Pick one this week and give it a try. If it doesn't feel right or seem to be helping, try another. Don't give up before you find a couple tricks that work for you!

1. Talk to a counselor.

2. Check your self-talk.

3. Remind yourself of the truth about your situation.

4. Ground yourself in reality.

5. Accept the things you cannot change.

6. Change the things you can.

7. Set and keep healthy boundaries.

8. Choose joy, peace, and fun.

9. Keep a good perspective on life.

10. Keep learning and growing.

Download and print this list at
https://davidedwardcummings.com.

The Serenity Prayer begins with one of the most powerful principles in personal wellness: accept the things you cannot change. Much sleep is lost over things that are out of our hands: wayward kids, callous spouses, merciless bosses, and terrifying politics. Accepting what we cannot change doesn't mean we stop caring – it simply means we stop agonizing over those things and give them up to God. How much of your anxiety or depression is rooted in things that you cannot change? One of the most upsetting things we can't change is the inevitability of change itself. I can agonize over the fact that my boys will soon be leaving home for college in a and that a very important era of my life is coming to an end, but where does that get me? The sooner I accept the fact that change is inevitable, and that I can't do a thing to stop it, the sooner I can get on with the business of enjoying what's in front of me right now.

6. Change the things you can.*

It is very tempting to play the victim role. Maybe you are a bona fide victim, but being a victim as a lifestyle has never helped anyone to recover the life of joy and peace that they long for. First, make a list of things you could actually change if you really wanted to – be honest. Then decide which ones you are willing to change. Change usually comes at a price – what price are you willing to pay? Your list may include the possibility of changing jobs or moving to a new city. It may center around changing your hobbies, activities, friend groups, or the church you call home.

If we're honest, there are very few aspects of our lives that we really can't change. We can't change the past. We can't change other people. And under most circumstances, we should not try to change the person we're married to. Besides those, little else is set in stone. So what do you wish was different, what would need to be sacrificed to make those changes, and is it worth it? Hiding, isolating, burying your head in the sand will not make problems go away. Wishful

---

*I don't generally condone using the Can-Change List as an excuse to give up on your marriage. Most marriages are difficult. If yours seems too onerous to continue, please consider seeing a marriage counselor before throwing in the towel. With the possible exceptions of significant toxicity or abuse, many marriages have a fighting chance with professional help.

thinking will not make problems go away. Take decisive action to fix things that are within your reach.

When I was having panic attacks in Costa Rica, I changed what I could: I left. I went home and got help. It seemed nearly impossible at the time. It seemed like I was just going to have to power through the panic. But I took a stand for my health and did what I needed to do. You can do the same.

7. Set and keep healthy boundaries.

Good boundaries are like the GPS in your car or on your phone – they keep you on the right road when you're not really sure where you are. Learn to say no to requests (or demands) placed on you by others that take you off course. Sometimes this means saying no to things that are essentially good, but not necessarily good for you right now. This allows you to say yes to the things that are most important to you. No matter what you've been taught throughout your life,
you have every right to set personal boundaries. You have the right to choose what you eat, where and when you go, how to dress, and how to run your own life. You have a right to have a say in all and any matters that affect you. You also have the right to choose who will and who will not be allowed to have a voice in your life, including how others can treat you and speak to you. Your wants and needs matter as much as anyone else's.

Establishing your own boundaries are a basic right given to you by God Himself, and absolutely no one has the right to take that from you. It requires some assertiveness, and it may produce conflict, but in the long run, clarifying your values and setting boundaries to protect them is a critical piece in your story of personal wellness. By setting and keeping clear boundaries you will be better able to manage your time and commitments, express yourself without fear of judgment or retaliation, surround yourself with people who will speak words of life to you, and take control of the direction of your life.

Nudges[4] are a useful twist on boundaries: where boundaries tend to say no, nudges encourage yes. If you are trying to learn the discipline of eating healthy, you may set a boundary that says no cookies are allowed in your house. A nudge goes one step further

138

and puts carrots on the counter where you will see them and want to snack on them instead of pining for the cookies. Start with boundaries but let them evolve into nudges.

HOW YOU THINK ABOUT YOUR STRESSORS ULTIMATELY DETERMINES HOW YOU RESPOND TO THEM MENTALLY, EMOTIONALLY, AND PHYSICALLY.

---

8. Choose joy, peace, and fun.

The key word here is *choose*. You have the right to be happy and enjoy life, but if you've struggled for long, you may have come to believe that those things are for other people, not for you. You need to begin looking for opportunities to laugh again and to enjoy each day, and then act on them. Push back against feelings of guilt that you may feel with fun and pleasure.

When life bears down on us, our activities and hobbies often suffer. We don't have the time, we reason, for something so trivial with all of the chaos around us. But not only do you deserve those enjoyable activities, you need them. Maybe it's time to start them up again, or develop new ones better suited to your current lifestyle. Life has to be more than work and struggle.

What did you love to do in the past? Find a way to do it again. If you can't go back to those old activities, then it's time to create new ones. Joy, peace, and fun are not merely the products of your circumstances. They are the products of your choices. Choose to forgive. Look for excuses to laugh. Seek humor. Be creative – everyone needs a creative outlet, not just the artsy types. Creativity can be art, writing, music, problem solving, yard work, house maintenance, working in the shop or garage – the sky's the limit when it comes to creative outlets. Small blips of enjoyment, when recognized consciously, can fill up your happy tank and build resilience. Find small daily refuges, places to hide or reset, like taking a walk in the middle of your day or sitting on the front porch with a book for fifteen minutes when you first get home from work. Let your mind wander every now and then to bigger refuges too – looking forward to summer vacation, or remembering your last visit to the family cabin – as a calming technique. Find your "happy place." The adage "whatever doesn't kill me makes me stronger" might have some truth in it, but from a psychological perspective, it is the enjoyable, safe, peaceful, fun experiences that build resilience, not the experiences that bring us to the edge of despair. Seek ways to reset yourself often with joy, peace, and humor.

ACCEPTING WHAT WE CANNOT CHANGE DOESN'T MEAN WE STOP CARING – IT SIMPLY MEANS WE STOP AGONIZING OVER THOSE THINGS AND GIVE THEM UP TO GOD.

---

9. Keep a good perspective on life.

A key truth about the stress response is this: how we *view* challenges and how we *perceive* our personal resources for facing them makes all the difference in the world with respect to how we react and respond to stressors. Attitude is everything when we face a challenge. Avoid black-and-white thinking that says "if it's not easy then I can't do it." Avoid playing the role of the victim, which only leads to helplessness. Set realistic expectations of your life, yourself, and others. Reject your tendency toward perfectionism. Keeping a healthy perspective on life means seeing things realistically, as they are, no worse and no better. It means believing that God has indeed given you what it takes to face the challenges that will come your way. Keep this mind: How you *think about* your stressors ultimately determines how you respond to them mentally, emotionally, and physically.

You can read more about the role of perception in the stress response in Appendix A.

10. Keep learning and growing.

Don't waste a trial, failure, tragedy, or challenge by forgetting about it as quickly as possible. Learn all you can about yourself. How might you have protected yourself from or avoided this problem in the first place? What did you do well to cope with it? The same is true, maybe even more so, with triumphs. Identify what you did well in that triumph. What did you enjoy about this success?

How did it happen? What inner strengths did you call on? Find your strengths and acknowledge them even if they seem tiny.

The more often we experience the feeling of being safe, the more that "safe" becomes the default feeling. The more often we feel loved, the more that "loved" becomes the automatic thought. What do you want to become your automatic thoughts? Seek out those experiences, however rare they may be, and dwell on them. Repeating the experience that you want to become an automatic thought will eventually replace older, less desirable neurological pathways in the brain. If you automatically think that you are unworthy of good things, find those rare times when you feel worthy and camp out there for a while to let that feeling soak in. Start with small joyful experiences, like the feeling of hot water pouring over your body in the shower. Our brains have a feature called experience-dependent neuroplasticity – the brain changes with our experiences. Focus on the good ones and you will be able, over time, to replace the old automatic thoughts that were biased negatively with new ones, more positive ones.

Knowledge is power, and the more you understand your struggles and your options to manage them, the more you are in the driver's seat. Understanding your situation can also have the effect of de-mystifying your mental and emotional struggles. Simply naming a problem lowers the activity levels of the amygdala, which, as we learn in Appendix A, controls your stress level.

There are some very good books out there on our mental health, and there are some especially weak ones too. Be particularly careful with what you read on the internet since there is no accountability for what people can post. Try to read information from reliable sources like universities, health care systems, and even government websites; regardless of how you feel about our government, organizations like the CDC really do have our best health interests in mind. These sources tend to post information that is based on the majority of evidence available rather than someone's opinion, a gut reaction to a problem or solution, or a few outliers to the general trends. Choose what you read carefully, but do all you can to learn about how you are responding to stress, anxiety, and depression in your own life. Be cautious about self-diagnosis, but remember that knowledge is truly power when it comes to your personal wellness.

Continuing to work on resilience-building even when there is no immediate emergency is one of the toughest things to do. We often let our guards down after a crisis has passed, quickly forgetting how miserable we were and how desperately we need better coping and resilience skills. Be sure to keep your resilience-building efforts ongoing during both the good times and the bad to ensure that you are ready when life throws you a curveball.

The most important step, and often the most difficult, in building resilience is committing yourself to doing something, anything. In the middle of a trial, we usually just want it to be over so we can feel safe, happy, and healthy again. It's not surprising, then, that we don't typically continue resilience-building behaviors when we're not in the midst of a crisis. But this can be a very productive time, since it is when we have a respite from our problems that we can think most clearly and learn some of the deepest lessons from our struggles. Resist the temptation to do nothing!

Feelings of being overwhelmed, panicky, or hopelessly depressed are among the most painful experiences in life. We all face them at one point or another. Some of us seem to get stuck in these feelings more often than other people, but no matter what, we need coping skills to face the inevitable trials of life. In this chapter we've explored a number of psychological strategies that may help you deal with stress in the moment and to build resilience to it for the future. Remember, like any skill these will require practice in order to perfect them. So use them as often as you can, even when you are feeling good, so that when you really need them they will be right there, ready for you to use.

In the second "resilience workshop" we will look at physical, social, and spiritual strategies for dealing with challenges to our mental and emotional well-being.

* If you have thoughts of hurting yourself or someone else, get help right away. Those are not clear, rational thoughts that can be trusted. Call the National Suicide Prevention crisis line at 800-273-8255 to talk to a live counselor 24/7, free of judgment and free of charge.

THE RESILIENCE WORKSHOP PART II

Physical, Social, and Spiritual Strategies for Coping with and Building Resilience to Stress, Anxiety, and Depression

"The chief function of the body is to carry the brain around."
Commonly attributed to Thomas Edison

Good mental and emotional welfare requires that we care for ourselves in all aspects of our being: psychological, physical, social, and spiritual. Just as neglecting any one area can negatively impact all of the others, caring for each area can positively affect the other areas of your life. In the last chapter we addressed mental and emotional strategies for building resilience to stress, anxiety, and depression. In this chapter we will continue with the resilience theme and turn our attention to spiritual, social, and physical self-care strategies.

PHYSICAL SELF-CARE

1. Move your body.

The positive effects of aerobic exercise on stress, anxiety, and depression are probably better understood than any other coping skill. It has been shown to be a good distraction from negative thoughts. It reduces muscle tension, which tells the brain that all is well, leading to a lowered stress level. Possibly most importantly, it builds brain resources in the form of helpful – and lasting – neurochemical changes.

THE POSITIVE EFFECTS OF AEROBIC EXERCISE ON STRESS, ANXIETY, AND DEPRESSION ARE PROBABLY BETTER UNDERSTOOD THAN ANY OTHER COPING SKILL.

There is solid scientific evidence to show that exercise of any kind – aerobic or strength training – not only helps us to "blow off steam" and feel good *about* ourselves, but it also brings about chemical and structural changes in the brain that can undo the cellular damage of stress, anxiety, and depression as well as protect against further damage. Exercise raises our level of tolerance for stressors (*i.e.*, it builds resilience) so that when the inevitable challenges and struggles come, we can handle them in much healthier ways.

As a biologist I can tell you that it is abundantly clear that we are designed to move! We have legs built for running, especially long distances. Our bones become brittle if we don't engage them and challenge them with significant impact every day. When we stop moving, either by choice or because of some health limitation, every major body system loses efficiency – we gain weight, our heart has to work harder to get blood to our organs, our blood clots or plugs up

EXERCISE BRAIN CHEMISTRY FOR THE SCIENCE-MINDED READER

While there appear to be numerous neurochemical changes that take place during and right after exercise, a short list of them seems to have the biggest impact on our mental and emotional well-being.

1. Increased **serotonin** leads to an overall sense of calm and safety by calming the sympathetic nervous response in the brain stem, dampening the amygdala, counteracting cortisol, and improving function of the prefrontal cortex leading to clearer situation assessment and decision-making.

2. Increased brain-derived neurotrophic factor (**BDNF**), made in both the brain and exercising muscles, further increases serotonin production, increases antioxidants in the brain, increases neuro-protective proteins that aid in cellular recovery from stress, induces growth of new nerve cells, and decreases cortisol levels.

3. Increased atrial natriuretic peptide (**ANP**), produced by an exercising heart, also counteracts cortisol, calms the amygdala response, and decreases the excitatory effects of epinephrine.

4. Increased gamma-aminobutyric acid (**GABA**), the key inhibitory neurotransmitter, calms all nerves in the central nervous system, lowering their reactivity, bringing calm to the mind and body. GABA is such a crucial piece to this puzzle that it is a primary target for many anti-anxiety medications.

5. Increased **endorphins**, a class of central nervous system hormones that resemble morphine, calm the body, which in turn calms the brain.

6. Increased production of **dopamine** by specialized nerve cells has far-reaching effects including improved mood, sense of wellness, and attention. It also slows intestinal motility, reducing bowel irritability and nausea from stress.

* For more on the science of stress, check out Appendix A.

with cholesterol, our digestive tracts give us trouble, risk of infection increases, and our brains stop working as efficiently. Every part of your body – even your brain – is made to function at its best in cooperation with movement.

Dr. John Ratey writes, "toxic levels of stress erode the connections between the billions of nerve cells in the brain… exercise unleashes a cascade of neurochemicals and growth factors that can reverse this process."[1] He goes on to say that "[exercise] is simply one of the best treatments we have for most psychiatric problems."

Wondering where to begin? Start simple. If you are not particularly active right now, walk around the house every day for a week. Then build slowly from there. Don't compare yourself to anyone else – the *process* is what matters, not the product. I go to the local YMCA three times each week. I'm pleased with the physical health benefits, but I remind myself every time I'm there that my real purpose is the mental health benefits.

Exercise at the gym or in your home is good. When combined with fresh air and the sensory experiences provided by nature, it becomes awesome! For most people, being outdoors is calming. There's just something about the feel of dirt or grass under your feet, the breeze on your face, and the sun shining down on you that brings peace. Maybe it's a reminder that you are part of something very special, God's creation, and that the Creator of all of this specialness is amazing. Scripture seems to imply that God intends to use nature to soothe and heal us when we're wounded. In Psalm 23, King David, who had more reason than most to be stressed out, praises God for leading him to a place of peace amidst the life-and-death struggles he was facing.

> The Lord is my shepherd, I lack nothing.
> He makes me lie down in green pastures,
> He leads me beside quiet waters,
> He refreshes my soul. (Psalm 23:1-3)

Picture David, a king on the run from very real enemies who wanted him dead. Imagine the physical stress of constantly moving from place to place, hiding in caves and avoiding being seen in case an enemy spy spotted him and turned him over. Feel his psychological distress at knowing that he could be killed at any moment by his former king or his own son, in his sleep or while walking through the wilderness. Watch as he and his small band of men come into an oasis in the desert, kick off their sandals and drop their robes, reveling in the grass and cool water and shade. Pulling out his parchment and quill, he begins to overflow with praise for God, his protector and provider. God used nature to remind David that He loved him dearly and was always with him. In this natural oasis the Lord restored David's tired and tattered soul.

Even if you're not the "outdoorsy" type, God uses nature to restore us and remind us of His love and provision. You don't have to be backpacking on the Appalachian Trail to experience this revelation from the Creator. You don't have to climb El Capitan or raft down the Rogue River to draw closer to their Author. You can enjoy spending an hour at the local park, or walking around your neighborhood, or sitting in the privacy of your own backyard. Opportunities to be outdoors come every day, from a break at work to the walk from your car across the parking lot at the store.

Not surprisingly, studies in science and sociology support the idea that experiences in nature are good for the mind, body, and soul. Journalist Richard Louv coined the term *nature-deficit disorder* to describe what researchers report to be "the human costs of alienation from nature, among them: diminished use of the senses, attention

147

difficulties, and higher rates of physical and emotional illness."[2] In most cases there is no harm in getting outside, and you may be pleasantly surprised at its effects on your body, mind, and soul.

We were clearly made to move, so get up and do something – anything! Walk. Run. Shoot some baskets. Throw a ball. Ride a bike. Whatever your body will allow you to do without hurting yourself. Being physically active, though it can be the last thing you feel like doing when you are stuck, may be the absolute best thing you can do. And when you do get moving, keep telling yourself, "I'm increasing my serotonin, BDNF, ANP, GABA, endorphins, and dopamine!" Or if that's too much to remember, just repeat to yourself, "This is good for my brain! This is good for my brain!"

2. Breathe deeply.

Deep, slow, intentional breathing is one of the very best in-the-moment coping skills and is also very effective for building long-term resilience when practiced regularly. Calm breaths signal the brain that all is well in the world, and the more frequently we tell our brains that everything is good, the less likely we will assume the worst when a challenge arises. Deep breathing exercises raise our tolerance to stress, making us less reactive and more prone to remain calm under pressure. Deep breathing makes it tougher for the amygdala to set your alert level to a higher state of vigilance. Many experts offer different techniques for deep breathing exercises, but at their heart they all come down to long, slow inhalation through the nose, making sure the diaphragm is extending and the belly is growing, followed by long, slow exhalation through pursed lips. I like to count to ten breaths and start over again if I have time for more. Guided breathing meditations can be found in smartphone apps and various websites from reliable and trustworthy sources like hospitals and doctors' offices. Combined with grounding yourself in the moment with the five senses, daily deep breathing can be one of the most important intentional things you can do to build resilience. Stress causes us to breathe rapidly and shallowly, a strategy that gets oxygen to the bloodstream very quickly in an emergency but also reinforces the message that there is a threat to be overcome. Intentionally slowing down the breath and deepening it sends the

12 PHYSICAL, SOCIAL, AND SPIRITUAL STRATEGIES FOR BUILDING RESILIENCE

There are numerous well-vetted techniques for overcoming stress, anxiety, and depression available in published books. Some are intended to help you in the moment when an emergency strikes. Others are best for building resilience to life's challenges over the long haul. Most are very helpful for both. Pick one this week and give it a try. If it doesn't feel right or seem to be helping, try another. Don't give up before you find a couple tricks that work for you!

1. Move your body.

2. Breathe deeply.

3. Remove yourself.

4. Let it out.

5. Relax and reset.

6. Eat and drink wisely.

7. Consider medication.

8. Connect with safe people.

9. Serve others.

10. Pray.

11. Worship.

12. Reflect on Scripture.

Download and print this list at
https://davidedwardcummings.com.

opposite message to the brain – that everything is safe here, that we can reset the stress level to a lower state of alert.

Think of it this way: the brain is constantly sending signals to the autonomous organ systems – breathing, heart rate and circulation, digestion, and alert level – keeping them functioning in ways that are appropriate for the situation. At the same time, these systems are sending information back to the brain, telling it how things are going. The two go back and forth to come up with the appropriate physiological responses. You can consciously influence your breathing, and by intentionally slowing it down, the brain gets the message that the situation is safe and sends the signal to the other systems to calm down. By controlling your breathing during an episode, you can bring calm and clarity back to the situation. And the best part is, you can do brief deep breathing exercises pretty much anywhere and anytime. I do them on my long commute to and from work, or in the middle of a stressful department meeting. The effect of deep breathing is a calmer body and mind.

3. Remove yourself.

Depending on what is triggering your reaction, you may need to remove yourself from the situation. If a particular person is hitting all your buttons and you feel you are about to tip over the edge, walk away if you can. If your job responsibilities or other work-related stressors are pushing you to your limits, it may be time for a personal day or even a vacation. If you are wearing yourself out, it may be time to rest, slow down, or clear your schedule for a few days. Remember, your Can-Change List is generally much longer than you are willing to admit. When I was struggling in Costa Rica, I made the tough decision to pull out and head back home. While it felt like defeat at the time, my therapist helped me to see that it was in fact a victory because I had the good sense to make a tough decision and remove myself from the situation, despite my muddled thinking. I am not saying you should run away from all of your problems, but sometimes removing yourself from whatever is triggering a negative response can be a very helpful coping skill.

4. Let it out.

Studies have shown that one of the most important factors in how we respond to stressful situations is how we perceive our ability to let out our frustrations. Physical exercise, as described above, can be an excellent outlet with many positive side effects. If that's not an option in the moment, take a brisk walk, or find a private place to cry, yell, or punch something – preferably something made to be punched! (Let me remind you that it is never OK to direct your letting-it-out coping on any person. There is no excuse for verbally or physically abusing someone, even if you see them as the source of your problems. Letting it out should always take place in private.)

5. Relax and reset.

There are few more important ways to care for your mental and emotional wellness than getting a good night's sleep. For some reason, our culture has demoted sleep to a minor need at best, and often it is viewed as a weakness. The truth is, though, that God designed us to need sleep, and without it we do not function properly. Insufficient sleep has been linked to decreased learning, poor decision-making, increased anxiety, and more severe depression. Adults need seven to nine hours of sleep per night, and each individual falls someplace specific on that scale. So, if you need eight and a half hours, seven hours will not be enough despite falling within the recommended range. Let me challenge you: make good sleep a top priority for one week and then decide if it makes a difference in your ability to cope with stress and your emotional outlook on life. If you are not getting enough sleep even though you want to and are trying to, then you may have a sleep disorder; make it a priority to see your doctor and begin to solve your sleep problem. If you've ever raised a baby, then you know first-hand how difficult it is to function with poor sleep. My wife and I used to say, "If only we could get a full night's sleep, we could handle everything else this parenting gig throws at us." Maybe that was a little naïve, but sleep deprivation certainly did not help the situation. Get good sleep, and if you can't, get help.

In addition to consistent sleep, it's very important to establish a rhythm of rest in our lives. Experts say we should plan for a five-minute rest from our work every hour, at least an hour of rest every day, a full day of rest every week, and two weeks of rest every year. These are the minimum recommendations. So how do you actually pull that off? You have to (1) make it a priority, and (2) schedule it. If it's not a high priority for you to take breaks because you don't see the long-term resilience value in it, then things that claim to be urgent will take precedence and quickly fill up your time. If I'm being honest with myself, I have to admit that something is wrong with the way I'm scheduling my time if I don't have five minutes each hour to catch my breath and step away from my work.

Carve out an hour each day to take a break from things that are taxing your mind. And sleep doesn't count. We need an hour when we're awake, alert, mindful, and in the moment, without working, striving for something or agonizing over something, in order to reset ourselves. When we sleep, great things happen. But when we rest awake, other great things can happen. We need them both. Maybe plan something you can look forward to during the day – taking the dog for a walk, watching the NBA game on TV, reading a book, playing with the kids on the floor. Anticipating something enjoyable for that hour has the added benefit of brightening your mood during the work day and can give needed hope when you are discouraged.

In the Bible, God established the Sabbath long before we had healthcare professionals to tell us that we needed to rest for a full day every week. It's even included in the Ten Commandments. In the Old Testament we're taught that it should be a time of rest and worship. God even attached punishment to it as extra motivation for us to take it seriously. In the New Testament, Jesus added clarity to the Law, teaching us that the Sabbath is meant for our own good. We need it and God knows we need it, so He insists on it. As Christians, since we are under grace, and therefore under the spirit of the Law rather than the letter of the Law, we don't have to approach the Sabbath legalistically; instead we can humbly accept God's wisdom and provision for us and set aside at least one day each week to truly, fully rest from whatever it is we call work.

Finally, take time off each year from your work. Taking off one day every couple of months and calling that your vacation is not the same as taking a full week off, uninterrupted. It can take a few days off in row before you start to really let your guard down, before you stop thinking about everything you need to get done. Minimize use of your phone and email, avoid taking work calls or texts and emails, and intentionally shift your thinking to anything other than work. And as often as your mind wanders back to your work, gently guide it back away from work to other things, things that are restful and enjoyable for you. If you can afford to get out of town, by all means

152

put some distance between yourself and the things that keep you busy. If that's only going to add stress to your rest, then take a staycation. Sleep in. Go for walks. Do fun projects. Be creative. Go out to dinner. Take in street fairs and farmers' markets and live music and anything else that is restorative and distracting and unstressful for you. Like planning how you're going to use your hour of daily rest, planning a vacation can be exciting and give you something to look forward to during the rest of the year. Taking time off annually is a win-win situation all around.

Part of establishing a rhythm of rest includes rejecting our culture's pressure to move at a crazy busy pace. We need to consciously, intentionally reject crazy busy. Let the world move as fast as it wants. Reject FOMO (fear of missing out) by reminding yourself that no one can do it all, and you would make yourself miserable if you tried. Build margin into your time, your finances, and your mental space. Accept doing less and accomplishing less if it means resting and resetting more often and more deeply. Set limits and honor them. Accept that you are finite and simply cannot and should not try to do it all. Choose *quality* of life experiences over *quantity* of life experiences.

6. Eat and drink wisely.

We've already established that your brain and body are intimately connected. It shouldn't surprise you, then, when I tell you that poor eating habits can affect your mental and emotional state. When you habitually eat poorly, your body sends messages to the brain saying that you are unhealthy, which causes the amygdala to raise the alert level. Poor physical health, including poor nutrition, puts the body on higher alert status, raises stress levels, and increases risk of mental and emotional illnesses like depression and anxiety. Good nutrition, on the other hand, has been shown to increase our resilience in the face of stressors. These effects are likely due to numerous factors, among them a more positive view of ourselves – our self-worth, self-esteem, and self-belief. When we eat healthy, we are much more likely to believe in our own abilities to handle whatever comes our way.

Sugar and caffeine specifically have been shown to worsen symptoms of anxiety. Both of these chemicals increase our alertness and mental intensity, both of which are already supercharged when we're anxious. If you're dancing on the fringe of anxiety, your caffeine or sugar intake could be enough to push you over the edge. If you have a problem with these two vices, remember that they belong on your Can-Change List.

Let me illustrate this truth with a story from my own experience. I gave up caffeinated drinks – particularly colas and regular coffee – several years ago as part of a plan to manage headaches. One morning, before I knew I had an anxiety problem, I popped a K-Cup into the Keurig coffee maker and sat down at my computer while it percolated away. Like every morning, I added half-and-half and sipped at it while I got my work day started. As I tipped my mug to drain the last few drops, Ann took the used K-Cup out of the machine and said, "Oh, you decided to go back to regular coffee?" *Shoot. Did I really just down a whole cup of Peet's dark roast coffee? Well, I guess we'll see how it affects my headaches.* To my surprise, I didn't get any headaches. Instead, I had a panic attack. A couple hours after chugging my first cup of loaded coffee in several years, I found myself on the freeway in Los Angeles (which is stressful enough without caffeine!). I felt like I was going to cause an accident. I wondered if I could keep my car in my own lane, or if I could control my speed. *What if I couldn't stop the car? This is way too fast. I'm going to hurt someone.* If you've never dealt with panic attacks while driving, this might sound like crazy talk to you, but these were the strange and scary thoughts buzzing through my amped-up mind as I tried to make my way to LAX. I finally had to get off the road, eat some food, and pace in a parking lot for about an hour before I felt safe enough to get back on the road. The fear and panic only began to calm down a couple hours after that. At the time I didn't recognize it as a panic attack, but in retrospect it is very clear what happened: I was already on the edge of anxiety and the caffeine pushed me into panic.

Caffeine is probably less of a problem for depression unless you happen to have both depression and anxiety, which isn't especially uncommon. But the rollercoaster that sugar causes, first a burst of energy and an emotional high followed by a crash, can indeed worsen depression symptoms. The bottom line is that nutrition matters, and some foods in particular should be limited or cut out entirely.

7. Consider medication.

Your brain is far more complex and mysterious than your spleen, but it is not eternal and it is not *you* in the spiritual sense. If you wouldn't object to medicating your malfunctioning spleen, I'd encourage you to at least consider whether psychiatric medication might have a role to play in helping you to recover from your own personal mental and emotional health problems. People have mixed opinions about the value and morality of taking psychiatric medications. I understand and respect that, but my personal opinion as a biomedical scientist is that medications are appropriate when chemicals in the brain are not functioning as they were designed to function. Just as insulin may be required when our sugar processing chemistry is not working properly, psych meds may be helpful when our brain chemistry is malfunctioning. My only advice here is to discuss the possibility of medications with your doctor so you know what your options are. You can learn more about the main types of psychoactive medications and how they work in Appendix B.

SOCIAL SELF-CARE

8. Connect with safe people.

We were designed for relationships, first with God and then with other human beings. Yet, when we are struggling, our first inclination is to isolate ourselves. We convince ourselves that no one could understand what we are going through. We convince ourselves that we are broken and flawed and do not deserve friendships or the help of others. Pride may get in the way, leading us to believe that we can't afford to let others see us in this state, that people would no longer love or respect us if they saw this side of us. Nothing could be further from the truth. First, others might surprise you and actually understand; but even if they don't understand, safe people can at least empathize with you and lend a shoulder to lean on. Build a safe community around you. You need it more than you think.

Stop for a moment right now and ask yourself who is safe in your life. Who has earned the right to hear the details of your story? What relationships do you have that are sturdy enough to bear the weight of your struggles? If no one comes to mind, don't despair. You can meet people at church or other social organizations. If you're careful with the Internet, you can meet some wonderful people there who share similar interests. You can start building those relationships today. Go slow. Let it evolve naturally. You may be eager to have closeness with someone, but you need to let the relationship grow at its own pace. You'll know when it is strong enough to bear up under some of the burdens you need to share.

What do safe people look like? Safe people can empathize with you. They may not have had any similar experiences to what you are going through, but they can put themselves in your shoes and have compassion for what you are going through. A safe person never tells you to "just get over it."

Safe people are good listeners. They don't do all the talking or try to fix you. They offer limited advice at best (unless they are a professional mental healthcare provider).

Safe people don't reinforce your inaccurate thinking. If you are stuck in the victim role, a safe person doesn't act as a negative cheerleader, telling you that the world is out to get you and you don't need those losers and the system is rigged anyway. Likewise, safe people don't encourage unhelpful or unsafe behaviors like using alcohol or drugs.

DON'T WAIT FOR SOMEONE TO NOTICE THAT YOU ARE HURTING. YOU WERE NOT MEANT TO GO THROUGH LIFE'S STRUGGLES ALONE.

Safe people have good boundaries with you. That may seem counterintuitive at first, but a safe person doesn't become your punching bag or dumping ground. A safe person isn't available to you 24/7 to the exclusion of their own personal needs. A safe person sets limits on how much of your story they can bear with you.

Reach out to someone who will not judge you for struggling, someone who understands and accepts you. You need – you deserve – someone who will not reinforce your destructive behaviors, but at the same time will not judge you for where you are. If you don't have anyone safe in your life, begin building that community (*e.g.*, support groups). Resist isolation. Engage.

Whether you are naturally introverted, extroverted, or someplace in between, we all need people from time to time. When you are struggling, take the initiative to talk to someone, preferably someone safe. Don't wait for someone to notice that you are hurting. You were not meant to go through life's struggles alone. Resist the temptation to isolate yourself, which only leads to reinforcing negative thoughts and shaming voices. The Bible teaches that we are so much better off with a friend than trying to tackle a problem on our own (Ecclesiastes 4:9-12).

9. Serve others.

When you are feeling low, it is natural to think a lot about yourself. We are naturally selfish, especially when we don't feel right, but staying focused on yourself and your problems can only make matters worse. Find ways to serve others in your community. Volunteer to greet people in the lobby at your church. Read books to elderly people in the local nursing home. Join a park cleanup effort. Get out of yourself and into the lives and needs of other people. You may be surprised at the perspective it provides along with a developing sense of being OK. Of course, if your schedule is already crazy busy, then serving others may require some rearrangement of your calendar. If your calendar is filled with things that only serve yourself, then maybe it could use some rearranging.

SPIRITUAL SELF-CARE

When you are struggling just to get through the day, there is no better place to turn than to God because He knows you better than you know yourself. He created you with His own mind, heart, and hands, and knows exactly what you need to get through the crisis. Before anything else, I hope you'll hit your knees in prayer and praise. This is not a time to learn *about* God, or think *about* God, or talk *about* God. This is the time to connect with Him directly and personally, as a friend. This is the time to lean into your relationship with Him.

10. Pray.

The most basic and possibly the most important spiritual coping skill is prayer. Connect with your Creator, the Great Physician. This is the easiest and most accessible thing to do in times of crisis. You can be falling out of an airplane and be praying! You can pray in the middle of a difficult conversation or during a stressful meeting at work. You can pray in the quiet of your mind or out loud. Prayer doesn't have to follow a formula or sound impressive or theological. Prayer is just you reaching out to God. It can be as simple as, "Help!" If you're not sure that you believe God is there or that He cares, try something like, "God, if you're listening…" He can handle our doubts even in the middle of our prayers. Prayer is the ultimate expression of hope. Psalm 55:22 says to "cast your cares upon the Lord and he will sustain you." The very best way to cast your cares on Him is by talking to Him. What do you have to lose?

11. Worship.

The word worship comes from the old English word *woerthship*, meaning ascribing high value to someone or something, declaring its worth. Applied to God, that means that anything we say and do could be done with a heart of worship. We can sing songs of worship or speak words of worship. We can do silent acts of worship. Many have argued that a life of worship is our ultimate goal as Christ followers. The key in our current discussion is that however you worship, in song or spoken word or deed, make an intentional choice to declare God's immeasurable worth to Him, to revere and adore Him.

Why worship in the middle of a crisis? Well, for one thing, it's what you and I were made to do (*e.g.*, Psalm 150:6). It's *home base* and a *refuge* for our souls. Worshipping God turns our hearts outward, away from ourselves and toward the Creator. In the process, it is humbling, and humility is necessary for good spiritual health, which is necessary for good mental and emotional health. Pride, on the other hand, is a barrier to prayer and worship, a barrier to humility, and a barrier to well-being. Try writing down a few lines of worship on an index card, either words from your own heart or lyrics to a worship song that you find particularly moving. You can also find plenty of words of worship in the Bible – start with the Psalms if you're looking for words to put to worship. Carry that index card around with you, and then pull it out the next time you find yourself in a dark place. You'll see just what the light of worship can do!

WORSHIP IS HOME BASE AND A REFUGE FOR OUR SOULS.

---

12. Reflect on Scripture.

God's Word, especially promises in the Bible, can be sources of peace and perspective in times of trouble. If you're disciplined enough, memorize verses from Scripture that specifically point you to His love for you and His goodness so you can bring them to mind in the midst of trials. I'm not very good at memorizing, so to help myself along in this endeavor, I often make my various computer passwords a reference from the Bible. When I log in to a website with the password, I pause and recite the verses I'm trying to memorize. Keeping a Bible handy can also be very helpful. Put one in your desk at the office and another in the glovebox of your car. Download a Bible app to your smartphone. Do whatever you have to do to make sure God's Word is handy and accessible when you need it at a moment's notice. Think ahead of time about what passages you'd like to have at the ready in a pinch, and bookmark them so you don't have to come up with them on the spot.

Prayer, worship, and reading Scripture are the fundamental spiritual disciplines. Think of prayer, reading Scripture, and worshipping God as the first priorities of spiritual health. These disciplines will require a lifetime of practice, but they will pay off in ways you never dreamed possible: peace, joy, contentment, and a closeness with the Creator unlike anything else. The best part is that you can start (or re-start) today! Spend time in God's promises, learning them until they become automatic thoughts. Invest in your relationship with God. Remember, our worthiness of God's love has nothing to do with our degree of brokenness or perfection, but it has everything to do with God Himself. He loves each of us, not because we are perfect, but simply because He has chosen to love us. It's that simple. Reach out. Pray. Open the Bible and see what God has to say to you through His Word. And declare to Him His worth in worship. You can listen to inspiring music or simply tell Him how much you appreciate who He is and all He has done.

Don't let anyone make you feel guilty about how often or in what manner you do these things. Push back against all-or-nothing thinking that says that if you don't read the Bible every day then you're a lousy Christian and you shouldn't even bother trying. There's no shame in being unable to "do devotions" every morning at 0-dark-30. Don't give up just because you fall asleep every time you try to pray. The important thing is that you find a rhythm that works for you. Just because you have let it slide for the past week (or month, or year) doesn't mean you can't just pick it up and try again. *There is no formula for how this is supposed to be done.* Keep in mind that there is tremendous benefit to you personally for reaching out to God in these ways, and let that be your motivation. This is no place for guilt or shame.

Some final thoughts...

Avoid numbing behaviors like drinking alcohol, using drugs, pursuing unhealthy sexual gratification, taking up smoking, going on a spending spree, or getting lost in the internet or television. You know a coping mechanism is unhealthy if it is unhelpful in the long run or simply trades one problem for another. Anything that hurts you or your relationships is unhealthy. If needed, distract yourself with non-addictive, non-harmful activities like reading a book, being creative, or investing in a hobby. But keep in mind that even "good" distractions can work against you if you become obsessive about them. Moderate exercise, for example, is known to be an excellent coping mechanism, but spending three or four hours a day in the gym may actually be counterproductive.

Many people find that writing down their thoughts in a journal can be very helpful. For one thing, there is no fear of judgment from a journal. This can be very important when you don't feel like you have any safe people in your life to share deeply with. Your journal won't try to fix you or make you feel guilty about whatever you are going through. Additionally, putting words on a page can be very helpful in figuring out what you are feeling and why. You can even bring it with you to a counseling session with a therapist or pastor and use some of your entries as starting points for discussion. And you can throw the whole thing in the fireplace when you no longer need it!

Remember, the most important step is to commit to doing *something*. Doing nothing changes nothing. Not trying brings the same result as failing. Be willing to take a risk. Open up. Be vulnerable. Admit your need for help and change. Then take action. Baby steps at first. Set realistic goals. Push back against procrastination – act now! You may be able to take a big step like making and keeping an appointment with a therapist. Or maybe you need to start smaller, like committing to getting out of bed before noon and brushing your teeth. Start with something, anything, that you can do and do it. Small successes will lead to bigger ones.

DOING NOTHING CHANGES NOTHING. NOT TRYING BRINGS THE SAME RESULT AS FAILING.

Taking good care of yourself keeps you ready when the inevitable trials and tragedies strike. Not all of these approaches will be right for your personality. Find the nuggets of gold among the dirt. Figure out what works for you, what resilience strategies you can relate to, and then begin to implement them in your own life.

Well-being requires that we care for our mental and emotional health as well as take care of ourselves physically, socially, and spiritually. Building lifelong habits of self-care can increase our resilience to the inevitable stressors and trials by calming our minds, making the amygdala in our brains less trigger-happy, and increasing our tolerance levels. The happiest and healthiest people are those who are intentionally taking good care of themselves in all of these areas, not neglecting any of them.

In the final chapter we are going to explore God's promises to us, His children, that we can learn, memorize, and apply to our stress, anxiety, and depression. When you're ready, just grab your Bible and turn the page.

MORE THAN CONQUERORS

Finding an Abundant Life in Christ

"In all these things we are more than conquerors through him who
loved us."
Romans 8:37

You and I were made for more.

Did you know that? Did you know that no matter where you are
on the spectrum of mental, emotional, and spiritual health, God's
plan for you is even better, even more? If you're in a dark place right
now, believe me – better yet, believe Scripture – God's desire for
you is so much more, so much better than this. If you're in a good
place right now, praise God for it and know that you were made for
even better.

It's important that we remember this truth: God's plan for us is
not one of lukewarm mediocrity or simply trudging through life. He
doesn't intend for us to live life defeated and empty. His hopes and
dreams for us – yes, God has hopes and dreams for your life! – do
not consist of weakness, ineffectiveness, loneliness and isolation, or
continual failure. His desire is not that we should live in a constant

state of fear and worry, stressed, overcommitted, and overwhelmed. No, we were made for so much more.

Jesus said that He came to give us an abundant life. Instead, many of us are experiencing a life of scarcity, to use Brené Brown's term.[1] A life where it seems like there's not enough of the things we need and deeply desire. Not enough money. Not enough time. Not enough love, peace, and friendship. A life of scarcity also means we have bought into the enemy's lie that *we're* not enough. Not pretty enough. Not skinny enough. Not smart, motivated, successful enough. Not good enough. Not Christian enough. This is not at all what Jesus had in mind when He chose the word "abundant" while speaking about the life He desires for us.

Made to *become* more

Have you ever reflected on your personal character and wondered if God's plan was for you to grow into something much more beautiful, much more like him? That's the Holy Spirit whispering to your heart, telling you that He has so much more in store for you than the person you are today.

When I was a young man, first striking out on my own, my only goal was to have fun. Up until that point, it seemed like everyone else was having a grand time except me. So when I left home after high school, my number one objective was to claim what was rightfully mine. I quickly got myself a fake ID so I could buy alcohol and made friends with the local pot dealers to make sure I could get ahold of something to smoke anytime I felt the urge. I surrounded myself with other like-minded people, people who seemed to be having the time of their lives, in the bars every night and at the beach every day.

This went on for several years until one day I realized that I didn't recognize or like the person I saw in the mirror. I was shallow, selfish, undisciplined, and aimless. I wasn't the kind of friend anyone could count on for anything; I lied whenever it suited my needs at the moment without regard for how it affected anyone else. Sometimes I even lied just for fun, making up stories about my past to make it sound exotic and exciting. I mean, who wants to be a good kid from a good family and a good neighborhood?

DEEP DOWN, WE KNOW THAT THIS ISN'T HOW IT'S SUPPOSED TO BE, BUT WE DON'T KNOW WHERE WE WENT WRONG OR HOW TO GET BACK ON TRACK.

This wasn't how life was supposed to turn out for me. I was supposed to grow up to be successful, happy, and confident. I was supposed to become that guy that everyone looked to for sage advice and help in their time of need. I was supposed to be the man of deep character, honorable and wise, a friend to all. Instead I was becoming a worm. My life was headed in the opposite direction I had always assumed it would take me. Something had to change. Surely, I was made for more than this.

Surely I was made for more than this.

In many ways, that's what has happened to us as adults. We've been derailed, but not necessarily by our poor choices. We've allowed our mental and emotional struggles to take us far off course, leaving us with the sense that we are not who we were meant to be.

It's true. We were made to become more than we are. We were made by God to be patient, kind, good, faithful, gentle, and self-controlled (Galatians 5:22-23). We were made to do good works (Ephesians 2:10), to make disciples (Matthew 28:19-20), and to be Christ's ambassadors of reconciliation to the world (2 Corinthians 5:18-20). We were made to become people who worship the Father in spirit and in truth (John 4:23-24).

Somewhere along the way we've gotten off course: we've allowed our struggles to become obstacles to becoming all that we were made for. Our anxiety and panic keep us from being the friend God intends for us to be. Depression holds us back from doing good works or reaching out to make disciples for Christ. Unresolved hurts, broken relationships, and unforgiveness make us angry rather than patient, harsh rather than kind and gentle. The guilt and shame of past and present sins hold us back from giving ourselves fully to worshipping God. We're disappointed in ourselves, disappointed in others, disappointed in how life is turning out. We make excuses for not attending weekend church services, excuses for pulling out of the weekly Bible study or never signing up in the first place. We avoid prayer because we are too ashamed of ourselves to face God. We don't feel worthy of speaking to the King of the universe.

Deep down, we know that this isn't how it's supposed to be, but we don't know where we went wrong or how to get back on track. We've allowed the roadblocks of life to take us so far off course that we can't even see the road anymore much less find our way back to it.

Something has to change.

Made to *experience* more

Every one of us was made to *become* more than what we currently are, and we were also made to *experience* more than what we are currently experiencing. When Jesus said that He came to give us life abundantly, He meant that He intended to bless us, among other things.

Did you know that you were made to experience more love, joy, and peace (Galatians 5:22-23)? Would anyone say that they wouldn't like to experience more love in their lives? Some of you are thinking that any love would be more love than you're experiencing today. God hears your cries for love, and He very much wants you to truly receive and experience His love and the love of other human beings. You were made for it, designed to thrive in it, and you'll wither without it. Studies in orphanages have shown that babies who aren't loved fail to thrive and sometimes even die, despite proper nutrition. It's in our DNA. God knows we need it more than almost anything else. So, if God's plan is for you is to experience great love in your life, what obstacles have you allowed to get in the way of finding and receiving that love? What positive steps can you take today to remove those obstacles so that you can fully experience the love that God so passionately wants for you?

For me, I never really felt unloved. My parents always made it abundantly clear how much they loved us kids, even during their separation and divorce. As an adult, for many years now I've had a wonderful wife who loves me unconditionally, without judgment or unfair expectations. My relationships with my kids have always been strong, even through the tumultuous teen years. I have good friends who have been there for me, showing me love in good times and bad. Beyond these human loves, though, I have generally felt loved by God. Yes, like anyone else I've experienced doubt and fears in my relationship with the Lord, but overall, I have believed that He loves me, even when my situation has seemed impossible, even when I haven't *felt* loved by Him.

Where I have struggled more is with a lack of joy and peace. As far back as I can remember, I've always been a serious person. When others are having light-hearted conversation – small talk – I'm the guy at the party who wants to talk about deep issues, serious issues. That's just my comfort zone. People have always told me that I need to lighten up (which is like telling a tiger to change its stripes – just saying). In the background of my heart there have always been low-lying clouds, a slight gloom, like a cloudy winter day when you can't really distinguish where the grey ground ends and the grey skies begin. Psychologists call this dysthymia, a persistent, low-level depression, always there, always hovering over things. Most of the time I can tolerate it or even overcome it under the right circumstances. But it's there, part of my experience. I've put it on my Cannot-Change List.

I'm grateful that it has become somewhat lighter as I've gotten older and grown as a Christian, but if I'm honest I have to admit that joy still does not come naturally to me. Maybe you can relate. My wife will tell you that I'm not the most playful person. Being tickled makes me angry rather than bringing on laughter. I don't usually seek out joy – I don't always feel worthy of joy, even though joy is a fruit of the spirit, a result of allowing God's spirit to abide in me and change me from the inside out. It's not that I don't *like* joy – when I do get to experience joy, I am thrilled and grateful and inspired and overflowing with hope. It just doesn't come easily for me.

Yet the Bible says that we are made to experience joy, more joy than we have ever experienced. And not just when we get to heaven, where joy will rule our hearts, but right here on Planet Earth. Happiness, it has been said, comes and goes with our circumstances. Joy, on the other hand, runs underneath our circumstances, like a current of water flowing beneath the waves. No matter what the waves are doing at the surface, joy flows steady and unchanging, like the One from whom the joy originates. Joy sticks around even when the happy experiences are over.

I want that joy. God wants that joy for me. Shame tells me I'm not worthy of that joy,and that I don't deserve it because it's meant for others, not me. God's Word says otherwise. I *choose* to believe God's Word over the voices of shame in my head. I choose to identify my joy-obstacles and remove them as often as they appear. I choose to pursue the joy that is rightfully mine in Christ.

In addition to joy, you and I were also made to experience peace and contentment (Philippians 4:7, 11-13). I've often thought that so much of my own struggle and pain in life would be alleviated if I could find true contentment. Financial worries would all but disappear if I could learn to be fully satisfied with God's provision for me. Relational difficulties would cease if I could contentedly accept the people in my life just as they are and let God worry about their character and flaws. Even my own anxiety and depression would be less intrusive, less of a threat, if I simply accepted them, radically accepted them, as part of my experience on this broken globe.

As we saw in Chapter 11, the Bible is far from silent on the issue of contentment. Jesus said that joining contentment with godliness creates the perfect combination (1 Timothy 6:6). He also said that we need to make His priorities our priorities if we want to be content (1 Timothy 6:11). We are taught to seek after God and be content in everything else, trusting that He will meet our needs (Matthew 6:33). The apostle Paul even goes so far as to say that we should seek to be content with nothing more than clothing for our bodies and a roof over our heads (Philippians 4:11-13). I have to admit, contentment is a tall order for me. I want more of everything, and I want it yesterday. But I am convinced that contentment is a virtue worth pursuing, and I plan to keep on seeking after it.

The main reason I so desperately desire contentment is that true, real, deep, honest contentment brings peace, and I want peace more than anything this world has to offer me. I bet you do, too, if you stop to think about it. Did you know that your marriage is actually meant to be a place of peace? Maybe it's difficult to believe if it's a place of strife and battling, but it's true. Your marriage, your other family relationships, your friendships, your life at work, your life at church – all of these relationships have the potential to bring peace rather than stress and frustration. God's plan for our lives includes peace, a deep abiding sense that all is well, even in the midst of turmoil. We're all human, so our relationships are not going to be perfect, but that doesn't mean that they can't be covered by peace. In many ways, peace is like joy in that it is not dependent on circumstances. Life circumstances will rise and fall like waves, but peace can remain constant despite our circumstances.

Peace says that you will be OK, even though your wife just announced that she is leaving you and the kids. Peace says that my family and I will have what we need even though there isn't enough money in the bank to cover this month's bills. Peace says that your loved one will spend an eternity in heaven in joy beyond joy, even though she is about to breathe her last breath on this earth. Peace says that no matter how turbulent life seems, the most important and eternal truths are still true.

My struggle with anxiety is called generalized anxiety disorder (GAD), meaning that it's typically an accumulation of many smaller stressors that cause me to become overwhelmed and anxious. My natural tendency is to assign too much weight to each stressor so that they quickly add up and take me to a bad place. In addition the GAD, I do have one specific phobia that causes me a lot of angst: I have a fear of flying. It's not the *idea* of flying that gives me trouble – as a scientist I am confident that the physicists and engineers have long since figured out how to make this six hundred-ton chunk of metal stay airborne at six hundred miles per hour nearly seven miles above the earth's surface. And it's not just due to claustrophobia or a fear of heights, though I think those two things factor in. For me, it's the turbulence.

I can be perfectly at ease sitting in my seat, reading a book or watching a movie on the back of the seat in front of me. Then it feels like we just ran over a pothole. But I know there aren't supposed to be any potholes up here. Then another pothole. Instantly my hands start sweating, my heart begins to pound, and my mouth goes completely dry. I become laser-focused, unable to pay attention to the movie or book, on high alert anticipating the next pothole. Soon it feels like we're driving this thing off-road. The fasten seatbelt sign lights up, the flight attendants go back to their own seats and announce that everyone must return to their seats because we've encountered a "rough patch" of air.

Rough patch, my foot. I know this is serious, that we're on the edge of losing control. I can just picture the pilot running around the cockpit, waving his hands over his head in chaos yelling "Oh no, turbulence! We're all going to die!" I know, it sounds silly, but this is where my warped fight-or-flight thinking takes me. You can tell me that turbulence isn't usually dangerous, just uncomfortable, but that doesn't really help in the moment. You can tell me that I was in more danger when I drove to the airport this morning than I am in right now, but that doesn't help me. I can look around the plane and observe people sleeping through the turbulence, sipping their coffee through the turbulence, reading a book through the turbulence. That doesn't help. In fact, I'm sure they are just oblivious to the danger we're all in, and I'm the only one on the plane with any sense in my head!

I start swearing off flying. *This is the last flight I take. I'm done with this. This is crazy.* I begin to wonder if it's possible to drive from California to Costa Rica. *How long would that take? Are there roads that actually go all the way through?* The only thing I can think of right now is planting my feet firmly on the ground.

It's interesting to me that my automatic response in this state of fear, the one coping behavior I always go to and the only thing that brings me any comfort, is to look out the window. I need to see the ground: steady, unchanging, solid rock. I need to know that underneath all of this turbulence, the world is still there, spinning and doing what it always does. That perspective helps me to see the turbulence a little more clearly, a little less dramatically. It helps it to feel a little less out of control. It helps me to know that in a short while, minutes or hours at the most, this turbulence will end, and I will in fact be back on solid ground again.

I've come to see turbulence as an accurate metaphor for life. When I'm cruising along at six hundred miles per hour, seven miles above the planet, I can feel safe and secure as long as things are going smoothly. As soon as a challenge hits – turbulence. Do I see the turbulence as minor and safe, or does it feel out of control? Do I honestly believe that I can handle it, or am I afraid that I don't have the resources to deal with it? Am I worried that the Pilot has lost control and all hope? Or do I believe that He still has it well in hand? The only and best thing I can do to cope in times of turbulence is to stare out the window at the solid rock beneath me. I have found that I need to spend more time reading, praying over, and believing God's amazing promises for my life. These are the solid rock beneath me during life's turbulence that can steady my soul and give me the confidence to press on.

While Scripture is chock-full of God's promises to us – promises to always love us, sustain us, provide for us, protect us, be with us, and so on – I find that Romans 8 says it all. Let's take a look at these promises together. I encourage you to go to my website (http://davidedwardcummings.com) and download the Made for More and More than Conquerors fridge notes. If, like me, you've spent a lifetime thinking inaccurate thoughts about yourself, life, and God, it is going to take time and repeated exposure to the truths of Scripture before you begin to actually believe them and let become your automatic thoughts. By pinning these up around the house – on the fridge, the bathroom mirror, the pantry door – you can continually remind yourself of the truths that matter most so eventually they will be in the very front of your mind every time you need them.

Paul starts the chapter with one of the most profound and life-altering statements in all of Scripture: "Therefore, there is now no condemnation for those who are in Christ Jesus" (Romans 8:1). Wow! Did you catch that? If your mind was not just blown, read that verse again, slowly. No condemnation. Ever again. I bet you've read that verse before. I bet some of you memorized it in AWANA when you were a little Sparky (AWANA is a Bible memorization club for kids, if you're scratching your head right now). Have you really, truly taken this statement as a simple matter of fact and allowed it to seep into your consciousness and subconsciousness, allowed it to change your view of yourself and the world and God Himself? No more condemnation. Nothing and no one judges you ever again.

No more external judgment from the world, at least none that actually has any power over you. No more judgment from your overly critical parents or that pastor that seems to be wagging his finger at you every Sunday morning. No more judgment from the voices in your head, voices from the past that tell you that you will never amount to anything, that you aren't worth a lick, that you're not pretty/funny/smart/popular/perfect enough.

NO MATTER HOW UGLY IT GETS, NO MATTER WHAT HORRORS YOU ARE FACING TODAY, HEAVEN WAITS FOR YOU ON THE OTHER SIDE OF IT ALL.

And most importantly, no more eternal condemnation for sin. The Bible teaches us that our sin, our stubborn rebellion against God and refusal to do things His way, separates us from Him. No amount of good deeds can outweigh even the slightest of sins on our record, but when we willingly unite our fate to that of Jesus (what the Bible calls being "in Christ"), all condemnation for our sins, all deserved punishment and eternal separation from the Father, is wiped out, clean, as if it never happened. No condemnation for those who are in Christ Jesus. If that doesn't get your pulse racing with excitement, you should probably see a doctor! That has to be the best news, the *good news*, in all of Scripture. When turbulence hits, I can remind myself that I am no longer condemned by the world, by my own thoughts, or by God, and that the judgment and punishment that accompany condemnation are a thing of the past.

As if this incredibly wonderful news is not enough, Paul goes on to tell us that we are God's adopted children, chosen by the Father to be the sons and daughters of the King. And as sons and daughters of the King, then we are the heirs to His kingdom.

For those who are led by the Spirit of God are the children of God. The Spirit you received does not make you slaves, so that you live in fear again; rather, the Spirit you received brought about your adoption to sonship. And by him we cry, "Abba, Father." The Spirit himself testifies with our spirit that we are God's children. Now if we are children, then we are heirs – heirs of God and co-heirs with Christ, if indeed we share in His sufferings in order that we may also share in His glory. (Romans 8:14-17)

In fact, Paul argues that the glory of heaven is so far beyond anything we could ever imagine that our struggles in this life won't even compare. "I consider that our present sufferings are not worth comparing with the glory that will be revealed in us" (Romans 8:18). In heaven we will never look back on the trials of our earthly life and stew on past failures and pain. As low as we can get here on earth, heaven will be so much higher that we will never look back with regret or even painful memories.

No matter how bad things are or how bad they may get, in the end we inherit an eternity of peace and joy beyond belief. In the end, we win. No matter how ugly it gets, no matter what horrors you are facing today, heaven waits for you on the other side of it all. Wow. Close this book for a few minutes and let that truth sink in.

In the 1992 preface to his classic book *Man's Search for Meaning*, Auschwitz survivor Viktor Frankl claims that Hitler's concentration camps taught him that life always has meaning, no matter how bad the circumstances.[2] He writes, "life holds a potential meaning under any circumstances, even the most miserable ones." By "the most miserable ones," he means degradation and humiliation, torture, daily threats of death, starvation, frostbite, and bearing witness to horrors and atrocities that would lead even the most devout Christian to wish every hour for his own death just to end the suffering. After all he had experienced and witnessed, Frankl nevertheless concluded that life does not lose its eternal meaning, and the promises of God do not fail, fade away, or become void, in the face of difficult circumstances. Considering all that he had been through, this is an astonishing confession.

In Romans chapter 8 verse 28, the Bible teaches us a truth that may be one of the most difficult for us to accept: God can and always does bring about good from the bad. "And we know that in all things God works for the good of those who love him, who have been called according to His purpose" (Romans 8:28). Two very important questions emerge from this teaching:

First, does this mean that God *causes* the evil in this world? This is a critical question for us to sort out because one of the most common reactions we have when we or someone we love is suffering is to ask God why He would do this to us.

- Why would you give my husband cancer, God?
- Why would you take my job away from me just when we need the money most?
- Why would you make me go through life with depression?
- Why must I have panic attacks, God?

The Bible tells us that God cannot even be tempted to do evil (James 1:13), much less to actually carry it out. Furthermore, it tells us that God is nothing but good (1 John 1:5). No, if God was the source of evil in the world then He would not be God. When we begin to believe what the Bible teaches about God's character, then we can stop blaming Him for the bad things that happen to good people, and we can turn to Him for help.

EVEN IF YOU NEVER SEE THE BENEFITS OF YOUR STRUGGLES, YOU CAN REST ASSURED THAT THE FATHER IS REDEEMING THEM FOR YOUR OWN GOOD, THE GOOD OF THE PEOPLE YOU CARE MOST ABOUT, AND PROBABLY EVEN THE GOOD OF COMPLETE STRANGERS YOU WILL NEVER MEET IN THIS LIFE.

The second question we need to address is this: Does everything happens for a reason? I often hear people make this claim, especially when something really difficult happens. I understand the desire to believe it is true: if everything happens for a reason, it's easier to believe that your difficult situation is going to work out just fine in the end.

I'm not convinced.

From my studies of the Holy Scriptures, I believe that the tragedies and trials we face in this life break the Father's heart just as much or even more than they break ours. Sin and the consequences of life in a fallen world, one in which the enemy is still on the loose, were never part of God's original plan. Natural evil – tornadoes wiping out entire communities, hurricanes displacing people from their homes, famines, epidemics, and everything else that doesn't appear to be directly due to human sin, is more difficult to understand. But I do believe that God has the power and the love to take even the worst of situations, the darkest and ugliest of evils, and use them to build His kingdom. Even if you never see the benefits of your struggles, you can rest assured that the Father is redeeming them for your own good, the good of the people you care most about, and probably even the good of complete strangers you will never meet in this life.

Paul ends this mini-sermon in chapter 8 with the assurance that absolutely nothing in the entire universe can alter or take away or nullify these eternal promises from God.

Who shall separate us from the love of Christ? Shall trouble or hardship or persecution or famine or nakedness or danger or sword... No, in all these things we are more than conquerors through him who loved us. For I am convinced that neither death nor life, neither angels nor demons, neither the present nor the future, nor any powers, neither height nor depth, nor anything else in all creation [nor any other turbulence we may fly through!], will be able to separate us from the love of God that is in Christ Jesus our Lord. (Romans 8:35, 37-39)

To be sure, life can be hard. But God's promises will always stand.

Never again will we be touched by the sting of condemnation.

Heaven's perfection waits for you and me after this imperfect life because we are adopted sons and daughters of the Most-High King.

The pain we experience in this life is not wasted – God will redeem every tear, every cry for help, turning it around for good.

And nothing, absolutely nothing, nullifies a single one of these promises. Not pain, not failure, not sin, not death. Not even the Nazi concentration camps can take away the eternal meaning of life and the love and promises of God.

Yes, you and I were made for so much more. More love, more joy, more peace. We allow our struggles to become obstacles to experiencing that love, joy, and peace, but we have the eternal promises of God to steady us in the midst of the turbulence. And nothing will ever take those promises away.

Afterword

Everybody's Got Bears

The black water pushed heavily against my thighs, threatening to knock me over and sweep me away into the brisk current. I spread my legs a couple inches further apart and twisted my feet, digging my wading boots deeper into the sand and cobble bottom. The icy river collapsed the neoprene waders around my legs, reminding me that it was September in Montana.

After re-establishing my balance, I lifted my fly line off the surface of the water and into the air. A few false casts to dry the fly and let out a bit more line, and the #16 elk hair caddisfly alighted onto the water upstream of me. As the current brought the fly toward me again, I stripped the excess line off the water and let it pile up at my side. I watched the tiny lure drift, bob, and swirl on the water, mending the line to keep the current from dragging the fly with an unnatural motion. There was no sign of the trout that had curiously nudged my fly a few casts before. It must have moved into a different feeding lane looking for something other than the caddisfly I was offering.

I tucked my rod and reel under my arm while I thought about my next move. Looking up from the water I took in the grandeur of the scene around me. The Absaroka range loomed high over my left like ancient cathedrals paying homage to their builder. Directly upriver from me, enormous mountain peaks in the distance parted to allow the mighty Yellowstone River to spill out of its namesake national park. Late summer cumulus clouds gathered from all sides, threatening to pour chilly rain on our expedition.

Deciding that we might have better luck if we covered more water, we climbed into the drift boat and pushed out into the middle of the river, quickly drawn into the fast current. One person took the oars while the other two made quick casts to either side of the boat.

If we missed a rising fish there was no time to cast to it again. We just had to lift the line out of the water and offer it up to another fish.

The current quickened as the channel narrowed, the Absarokas closing in on us. To the east, the foothills were still dominated by lodgepole pines, but a high berm dotted with spruce rose to the west. As we swept past the shoreline, a large, dark mass lumbered among the spruce along the river as if trying to keep up with us. It was a bear, and it was probably doing the same thing we were doing: fishing for a trout dinner.

Unlike my first encounter with a bear all those years ago in the sequoias of California, I wasn't frightened by this bear. I wasn't even startled. In the first place, I was a safe distance away, on a boat in the flow of a wide river. If we had been on foot on the shore I might have been on higher alert. But I could see that, although there was a bear just feet away from me, there was very little danger. Besides seeing the bear from a safe place, another important reason that I wasn't afraid is that I wasn't alone. I was with three friends, and I knew that the bear didn't stand a chance against all of us if we stood together.

We can and should expect to encounter bears from time to time. That's part of the price we pay, the risk we take when we live life on this earth. But they don't have to catch us off guard in the middle of the night. It's not necessary that they walk right up to us, forcing us to take a stand or run for our lives. We can learn to keep them at a safe distance. We can see them for what they really are in the clear light of day. And when we have people in our lives who are on our side, we can bravely face down the bears of stress, anxiety, and depression in our lives to find an abundant life in Christ.

Connect with Dave

Subscribe for weekly Mental Health Reminders and other updates:
https://davidedwardcummings.com/subscribe

Follow Dave on Facebook or Instagram @DavidEdwardCummings.

Please share the book website with the people you care about:
https://everybodysgotbears.com

For videos and other resources, visit Dave's website:
https://davidedwardcummings.com

Share your story with Dave: david@davidedwardcummings.com

Book Dave to speak at your event: david@davidedwardcummings.com

A small group curriculum to go with this book will be available Fall 2019.
Subscribe at the link above to be the first to know when it comes out!

Acknowledgements

To my wife, **Ann Cummings**. Your inexhaustible love and support made not only this book possible, but you have made my recovery and subsequent ministry a reality. I love you most.

To my kids, **Sydney, Ryan, and Joshua Cummings**. Your deep grace and acceptance of me during the most difficult times of my life have been the light of Jesus to me. I know Him better because of you.

To my church family at **Pathways Community Church** in Santee, CA. Through this entire journey you have been by my side, supporting and accepting me and my brokenness. Thank you for everything you have done and continue to do to share the love of Christ with a world in need.

To my work family at **Point Loma Nazarene University** in San Diego, CA. You have been my family away from family, my home away from home. Never once did I hear a condemning word, never a "should" with regards to my struggles. I love doing ministry with all of you and couldn't imagine a better group of colleagues to ride the ups and downs of professional life together with.

To my sister **Aimee Cummings**. You captured my thoughts beautifully in the cover art, and your unmatched editing skills have made this a much better book. I'm so grateful. Love you, sis.

To **Mike Johnson**. You have inspired me with your own life and writing. And you have been
a very practical help and encouragement in the process of making this book a reality. Thanks for your friendship.

To **Dave Bruno**. You never stopped telling me that this book was an important idea that needed to see the light of day. When the agents and publishers all turned me down, you always told me to keep at it, that it was worth it. Thank you for all of the wisdom you've provided and for your friendship.

To **Darrel Falk**. You are such an accomplished teacher, speaker, and writer. Your experienced guidance has been invaluable to my thinking about these issues and the importance of sharing a life-changing message with the world. You have challenged me to take this topic to the next level, and this book and ministry are vastly better for it.

To **Dean Nelson**. You've been a source of constant encouragement, even during the most discouraging times of writing this book. Thank you for all you have done for me and for all you have done for writers and journalists everywhere.

To **April Cordero** and **Dawne Page**. Thank you for your support and friendship. Your comments and suggestions made this a better book.

To **Denise Nelson**. I thought I was good with grammar and punctuation until you got ahold of the manuscript. I truly appreciate the time you poured into cleaning up my sloppy writing. Thanks for making me look good.

To **Kathy Moratto** and the wonderful people of **Set Free** at **Emmanuel Faith Community Church** in Escondido, CA. You have welcomed me into your family of honest, vulnerable people who love the Lord and want to grow. I can't thank you enough for trusting me to share my stories with you and teach you the lessons I have learned along the way. I have learned more from you than you know!

To **Mike Marino**. Your book *Freedom from Anxiety and Depression* has had possibly the biggest impact on my own recovery and thinking about our mental and emotional handicaps. Thanks for the help, encouragement, and wisdom.

To **Jesus** my savior. There are no words to describe my gratitude to you, Lord, for saving me, for calling me your own, and for using my life. You are everything to me.

Appendix A

The Science of the Stress Response

In the opening chapter of this book I told you a story about my first encounter with a bear in the woods. It was absolutely terrifying, but my stress response, also known as the fight-or-flight response, did exactly what it was supposed to do and kept me alive in the face of a very real physical threat to my survival. You may face life-threatening situations once or twice in your lifetime, but for most of us, the most dangerous thing we do is drive to work. Why do we still experience fight-or-flight from time to time? It turns out that psychological stressors can trigger the very same response as a physical threat like meeting up with a bear in the middle of the night. If we're going to try to understand why stress affects us the way that it does, we need to start with the brain and body physiology of the fight-or-flight response.

Maybe you've asked yourself one of these questions:

- What causes all of these mental, emotional, and physical feelings when I'm stressed out or anxious?
- What is going on in my brain and body?
- Is this normal?
- Can a panic attack give me a heart attack and kill me?

These are legitimate questions that most of us ask when we are struggling through significant challenges.

As a biologist, I have to write a chapter on the scientific aspects of the stress response. My intention is not to make you an expert in stress biology or to give you knowledge that will let you diagnose and treat yourself. I strongly suggest that you leave those things to the actual experts. Having a basic understanding of what is going on in your brain and body, however, can have many benefits. Here are just a few reasons you might want to read this appendix:

- Understanding what your brain and body are doing during a stress response takes away some of the mystery and therefore some of the frustration and fear.
- Simply naming a struggle takes away much of its power over you.
- Knowledge of the stress response gives us a framework for understanding how medications and other treatments/interventions might work (see Appendix B).
- Knowing that what you are experiencing is normal takes away some of the shame and stigma associated with mental health challenges.
- Knowledge can help you to develop more compassion for yourself and others.

What is the purpose of the stress response?

If you're still reading, then you must have decided that you want to know more about what you and others are experiencing. Let's start by addressing a very important question: Why do our bodies and brains respond to stress in this uncomfortable, sometimes miserable, way?

The stress response is often called the fight-or-flight response because it serves the fundamental role of helping us to survive a threat to our lives. When faced with a bear, it's important that we muster all of our resources for the task at hand, otherwise we may not live to see tomorrow. In a split second we need to decide whether to face the threat head-on (fight) or run away (flight). Either of these responses is going to take superhuman strength and speed to be successful. The primary goal of the stress response, then, is to prepare us physically and mentally to survive a physical threat to our lives.

There's another aspect to fight-or-flight that often gets left out: freeze. We really have three possible survival options when faced with a predator: we can fight it off, we can hope to outrun it, or we can go limp. That may sound crazy, but in some cases that is actually the best thing you could do. If a mother bear sees you as a threat to her cubs, she doesn't want to eat you and she isn't just being mean; she wants you to no longer be a threat so she'll try to chase you off or possibly kill you to protect her babies. If you know you can't possibly fight back and win, and if she's too close for you to out-run her, playing dead like a possum may actually be the safest option. Once she's convinced you're no longer a threat, she'll return her attention to her cubs and move them safely away from you. If you've ever frozen up in the face of major stress, then maybe you can understand this third option.

I once saw a news story on television about a river that had overflowed its banks in the Midwest during spring rains and snowmelt. People were underestimating the threat of the rising waters and many had to be rescued from their stranded vehicles. One particular woman was sitting on top of her car, which was mostly submerged in a violent, brown river full of trees and other debris. A hovering helicopter lowered a rope with a harness to pull her to safety. But when the rope reached her, she went completely limp and couldn't take the harness and strap herself into it. Eventually, a rescuer had to be lowered to the woman to assist her with the harness. When her rope was pulled up she just dangled there as if she was a corpse. When she was safe again on land and the emergency was over, she recovered her motor functions and was again able to move and sip a cup of hot coffee while being interviewed by reporters. Her brain chose option three, freeze, since neither fight nor flight were viable options.

More often than not, though, the body prepares to duke it out or make a 100-yard dash rather than play dead. And in either case, fight or flight, tremendous amounts of energy are going to be needed, at least in the short term. Not surprisingly, then, it appears that all of the rapid changes that take place in the brain and body are geared towards (1) mobilizing energy and oxygen to the brain and large muscles, (2) pushing the pause button on anything not absolutely necessary in the moment for survival, and (3) deadening pain and limiting inflammation.

Before we dive into some of the details, we need to understand that the stress response is relatively non-specific. This means that your brain and body go through essentially the same survival routine when faced with any perceived threat, whether you've just been

184

dumped out of the raft into the frigid raging rapids, or the mechanic just told you that it's going to cost you $1,000 to get your car back on the road. In either case, if you interpret the situation as a serious threat, the fight-or-flight response will begin. Let's take a look now at the process itself.

How do the brain and body respond to a perceived threat?

How we respond to life's challenges begins in the brain, and therefore *what and how we think* can make all the difference in terms of how our minds and bodies respond. In the case of a real physical threat, it makes perfect sense that we would recognize the seriousness of the situation and go into survival mode until the threat has passed. But what about psychological stressors, like financial worry or family conflict or stepping onto a stage to give a speech? Maybe you could make the argument that some degree of fight-or-flight – maybe focused attention or butterflies in your stomach – could be helpful in enabling you to rise to the challenge. But it's here, in the initial stage of the stress response, when our individual personalities and life experiences come into play. For example, as a teacher I have learned to not fear, even to enjoy, public speaking. Weird, I know. Financial worries, on the other hand, can completely derail me. Maybe you're the opposite. How we perceive the threat, how we think about the challenges we're facing, has a tremendous impact on the rest of the process. We'll return to this idea in a few minutes.

We're going to see that the brain and body are tightly linked together. The body can cause thinking and feeling problems, and our thinking and feeling can cause body problems. The tissues in your body are all made up of the same four building blocks: proteins, fats, carbohydrates, and nucleic acids (think DNA). Your brain is made of the same basic components as the rest of the body and therefore is subject to the same biochemical limitations and problems as your left foot or your eyeballs. The difference is that the brain is vastly more complicated than any other organ in the human body so we understand it far less. This lack of understanding shouldn't cause us to think of the brain in supernatural terms. Don't make the mistake of confusing your brain for your soul. I don't know what the soul is made of, but I'm pretty sure it's not proteins, fats, carbohydrates, and nucleic acids! Remember that problems in your brain are no more a reflection of you as a human being than problems with your kidneys or your liver.

So it all starts in the brain as we try to make judgments about our current situation in light of past memories. The main brain structure involved in setting the threat level is called the amygdala, a small structure buried deep in the core of the brain. In the 1980s movie War Games with Matthew Broderick, General Beringer had the job of setting the Defense Readiness Condition, or DEFCON, of the United States based on information he was receiving from the war machine, named after the son of its creator, Joshua. The amygdala is a lot like General Beringer: it continually evaluates information from the five senses, assesses that intel in the context of past experiences and knowledge, and sets your personal DEFCON level. If you are calm, relaxed, and handling things around you well, you might be at DEFCON 5 (the lowest level of vigilance). If you get a call from the principal's office at your son's school, maybe you have to raise your readiness to DEFCON 4. DEFCON 1 means you're ready for all-out war. Some people begin to experience the unwanted effects of stress like an upset stomach or migraines as low as DEFCON 4, while others have the ability to take it all the way to DEFCON 1 and still be on top of their game.

Based on the DEFCON level that your amygdala decides to set under a given set of circumstances, it may begin to alert the rest of the stress response system. There are two main branches of this system, one that relies largely on electrical nerve impulses and therefore responds very rapidly, and a second that relies more on chemical messengers called hormones and proceeds more slowly. In reality, both systems make use of both nerve impulses and hormone signals, but one, the sympathetic nervous system, is more weighted towards rapid nerve-based responses and the other, the endocrine system, uses slower chemical signals to achieve its goals. Combined, they are referred to as the neuroendocrine system, which is just a fancy word for the interactions between your brain and your hormones. Both of these systems are incredibly complex, but we're going to focus on the essentials.

The amygdala first alerts another nearby brain structure called the hypothalamus, which secretes a critical hormone called corticotropin-releasing factor, or CRF. CRF travels the short distance to the pituitary gland, also in the brain, causing it to release another hormone called adrenocorticotropic hormone (ACTH), which then travels the long distance to the adrenal glands located on top of the kidneys. ACTH stimulates the outer surface of the adrenals, the adrenal cortex, to secrete our first of three essential stress hormones, cortisol. This pathway represents the endocrine (slow) response to a stressor, requiring upwards of an hour before cortisol levels in the bloodstream become elevated.

The endocrine pathway is so slow that if we relied solely on cortisol to save us in an emergency, we'd all be dead! Fortunately, the amygdala also activates a neurological response, which is lightning-fast because it uses electrical impulses to activate key steps in the stress response. When the DEFCON level is raised a step, the amygdala can activate a portion of the nervous system called the sympathetic nervous system, which originates in the spinal cord. Sympathetic nerves do two things simultaneously. First, they send a message directly to the core of the adrenal glands, called the adrenal medulla, instantly inducing the release of a famous hormone called adrenaline, more commonly called epinephrine in scientific circles. Epinephrine is the second major stress hormone we need to know about.

The third stress hormone of the Big Three is called norepinephrine. It is released by the sympathetic nerves themselves where they terminate in organs and muscle tissues. Because norepinephrine is released faster than any of the others, it is probably responsible for the instantaneous physical sensations when we are startled by a jump-scare scene in a horror movie or frightened by turbulence on an airplane.

These three chemicals work together to prepare your brain and body for fight or flight. Remember that the main goal of this response is to mobilize and deliver high-energy molecules – mostly glucose – and oxygen to your brain and large muscles, as well as to shut down temporarily unnecessary functions. To mobilize energy and curtail superfluous activities for the moment, cortisol, epinephrine, and norepinephrine can have these effects:

Increased insulin. Insulin controls blood sugar levels by releasing stored glucose and by stopping the processes that store energy molecules like sugars and fats. It also ramps up a process called gluconeogenesis that creates sugars from fats. The total effect is that blood sugar levels shoot up in the blood during fight-or-flight in order to make this critical high-energy molecule available to cells that need to increase their function, especially the brain and large muscles. The long-term effects of increased insulin from chronic stress, however, may include muscle loss, weakness, and fatigue.

Increased respiratory rate. Eating and breathing work together to give us energy: energy is stored in food molecules, especially fats and sugars, and oxygen is necessary to break them apart and release the energy, much like oxygen is needed for a fire to burn. Extra sugars being delivered to the cells of the body are worthless without the oxygen necessary to break them down, so our bodies ramp up our breathing by increasing our respiratory rate. Fast, shallow breathing, labored breathing, or a feeling that your chest is heavy or that someone is sitting on your chest when you're trying to breathe are often a sign that you are under significant stress. Although it is uncomfortable, there are probably no harmful side effects to this part of the stress response.

Increased heart rate, heartbeat force, and blood pressure. Insulin makes sure that there is plenty of sugar available for the stress response, and the lungs and diaphragm work to get as much oxygen to the bloodstream as quickly as possible in order to support breaking down the sugars. Now the cardiovascular system – the heart and blood vessels – will do their level best to deliver all this precious cargo to all of the tissues and organs of the brain and body. This is often the most frightening physical sensation associated with the stress response. Countless people visit the ER because they are convinced they are having a heart attack because their heart is racing, pounding so hard it feels like it's going to burst. While this sort of response can slowly cause heart muscle damage and encourage the formation of atherosclerotic plaques in the blood vessels over the course of years, the medical community assures us that the risk of heart attack during a fight-or-flight stress response is miniscule for the healthy heart. It's mostly just uncomfortable and can be more than a little scary.

Decreased digestion. To understand this part of the stress response we have to remember that it is designed to save us from life threats that are very brief and very intense. One of the strategies, then, is to hit the pause button on processes that are unnecessary for survival when facing a predator or other life-threatening situation. While digestion is obviously important for long-term survival, eating and digesting food takes far too long to be of any use in an emergency, so the Big Three stress hormones temporarily shut it down. This means decreased appetite, saliva production, digestive enzymes, and nutrient and water absorption. It also means increased gut motility, a fancy way of saying that what is in your gut already is quickly ushered out without any absorption of nutrients. What you experience, then, is a dry mouth, an upset stomach (possibly including nausea or even vomiting, gas and bloating), and very often diarrhea. If the stress response is not reversed due to chronic stress, this part of the response can lead to significant weight loss, weakness, and fatigue. It is thought that a substantial number of IBS cases are due to chronic stress.

Decreased sex drive. Another expendable function during a life-threatening experience is the drive to reproduce. Apparently, you don't want to be thinking about sex when you're trying to avoid drowning or being eaten by a mountain lion. Go figure! Men often say that sex is a stress-reliever, while it is not uncommon for a woman to need calm and peace in her life to be receptive to a man's sexual advances. A woman's sexual desire may be more sensitive to stressors than that of a man. Related to sexual desire, stress hormones have been shown to decrease or even halt ovulation, to impede implantation of a fertilized egg in the uterine wall, and to decrease sperm production. More commonly, though, stress can also decrease sexual desire and interest, pleasure during sex, and the ability to have an erection or to reach orgasm. It is believed that most sexual dysfunction can be tied back to stress.

Inability to concentrate. When I faced the bear in my camp all those years ago, I couldn't have thought about anything else in that moment if I had tried. One of the mental effects of the stress response is to provide you with laser focus on the challenge. All of your mental capacities are zoomed in on this perceived threat to your survival, which is just what you need when facing a legitimate physical threat. When the threat is psychological, however, like a sick child or a dying spouse, the inability to concentrate on other things in life can be a burden and an obstacle to grieving and healing.

Inhibited memory and learning. Studies show that the formation of memories is inhibited during times of stress. This may be a result of shutting down unnecessary functions, or it may be a form of psychological protection. Imagine if we remembered all the details of being born! I have only foggy memories of the peak three or four months of my breakdown from a few years ago. A couple years later, I was talking with a close friend who lives several hours away and he mentioned spending time together then. He had flown here to see me and spent a few days at my house and I didn't even remember! Of course, since memory plays a large role in learning, stress can have a negative impact on our kids at school and our own ability to learn new information or new tasks on the job.

Elevated vigilance. Another characteristic mental effect of the stress response is an elevated DEFCON level. Increased vigilance – a heightened awareness of potential threats – is an important part of the fight-or-flight response. You may feel on edge or jumpy. Maybe you startle more easily, or you become more suspicious of unknown situations and unknown people. This increased vigilance is a defining trait of anxiety; when it becomes pathological, meaning that it interferes with the normal functions of life, it is deemed an anxiety disorder.

Hopelessness and helplessness. Sometimes, rather than elevated vigilance, the stressed-out person just wants to give up because the situation seems hopeless. They feel as though no coping mechanism can or will ever work for them. They accept a learned helplessness. They decline help from others and deny that any coping solutions could work for them. Their sense is that the stressors will continue forever and they will never get to experience peace and joy again, so they give up. This may be related to the freeze option of the fight-or-flight-or-freeze concept. No matter its source, hopelessness and helplessness are hallmarks of depression, a common mental and emotional side effect of chronic stress.

Effects on the immune system. We've all seen how much more easily we can catch a cold when we've been under duress. This is because the immune system is suppressed during the stress response. This may seem somewhat counterintuitive. If your life is being

190

threatened, you may be injured, in which case you are highly vulnerable to infection. Imagine being attacked by a predator – a bite wound can quickly become infected with bacteria, compounding the threat on your life. So why would the stress response suppress our immunity? Short-term stress boosts immunity, but that it then needs to bring it back down to baseline levels again or else risk a hyper-immune or auto-immune response, which would be equally dangerous. When stress lasts too long, the initial boost in immunity ends and the chemicals that return it to baseline levels (primarily cortisol) just keep dropping it lower and lower, overshooting the baseline and ultimately weakening immunity. Acute stress, which is what the fight-or-flight system is designed for, boosts immunity while chronic stress weakens it. A word of caution, though – the effects of stress on the immune system are probably not significant enough to allow anything more than a cold or maybe a flare-up of a cold sore. There is no evidence that stress-related immune suppression can make you susceptible to serious illnesses like cancer or hepatitis.

Why do some people seem to handle stress better than others?

Let me begin by first saying that many people around you who appear to be handling stress well are actually collapsing under the weight of it. This is especially true in environments where society tells us we are supposed to be having the time of our lives, like on the college campus or in the church. Due to stigma and other social pressures to keep it together, most strugglers will do anything to hide it. It never ceases to amaze me how often people confide in me, quietly with their tails between their legs as if they have done something wrong, that they are at the end of their rope, or that they are on medication but no one, not even their spouse, knows. Why do some people seem to handle stress better than others? Because most of them are faking it.

Having said that, there is in fact tremendous diversity in the human population for dealing with and responding to stress. Some people are more emotionally reactive than others. We've all met someone who collapses at the first sign of trouble, seemingly incapable of handling even the slightest challenge. Then there are those people who seem to thrive off of the most extreme challenges, never missing a beat. What makes one person so different from another? What makes you respond the way you do?

It won't surprise you to know that there's no easy answer to these questions. If we were talking about a relatively simple organ like your liver, we could explain most of how it functions and why, what outside forces impact the way it works, what causes it to break and how to fix it again. But this is the human brain we're talking about – the most complex organ, by far, in all of creation. There are no simple answers when it comes to this mysterious piece of engineering. But, by God's grace, we do know a little about it. Here are a few things to consider:

Genetics play a role in our predisposition to stress-related illnesses. How much of a role is debatable, but children of sufferers are more likely to become sufferers themselves, even if they are raised apart from their biological parents. Very likely, the genetic problems arise at the level of the various hormones we discussed earlier in the chapter, or the receptors on the surfaces of the cells that have to "hear" the messages the hormones are sending. When either of those components is broken, the hormone message or its receptor, illness ensues. Genetically inherited neurological problems also may play a part in increased susceptibility to mental health challenges. At least in theory, any hiccups in the neurological path or the hormonal path, can have consequences for the psychological health of the individual.

Prenatal stressors in the mother as well as stress and trauma in early childhood have both been shown to impact our ability to be mentally healthy as adults. The children of mothers who have gone through their pregnancies under extreme duress, such as in a war zone or experiencing abuse, are at increased risk of anxiety and depression disorders in childhood and adulthood. Similarly, children who are raised in traumatizing environments have a greater likelihood of developing stress-related illnesses later in life.

Related to early childhood stressors, we learn many of our coping strategies unconsciously by watching our parents and other caregivers as they cope with the messiness of their own lives. If dad deals with stress at work by having a drink or two every night in

192

front of the TV, the kids are more likely to automatically do the same. If mom deals with her loneliness by having sexual relationships with multiple partners, the kids are more likely to seek out serial relationships, as well. When no one is talking about their pain, fears, and struggles in the family, the kids learn that these are things to be ashamed of and keep them to themselves. When boys are told not to cry or made to feel that asking for help makes them weak, they will become men who don't know how to express their emotions or seek support in others. Like it or not, you and I were strongly influenced by how our parents dealt with life. If you are raising your own kids, remember that they are always watching, unconsciously picking up on your patterns and making them their own automatic responses, too.

Not surprisingly, a person's complex and highly personal history as well as current life circumstances can both have a tremendous impact on their ability to cope with the stressors of life, both big and small. For example, someone who has been fired from multiple jobs may have a hard time believing that she is capable of providing for her family, leading to fear and low self-esteem, while someone who has found great success in many of his endeavors may not find the prospect of a risky decision to be a significant threat. A single mom raising three young children in a small apartment in a tough neighborhood, working two jobs, and barely making ends meet might react differently to criticism from her boss than would someone in less trying circumstances would react. While just about any factor might play a role for one person or another, the most important seem to be the availability of time and money, family conflict, job satisfaction, and disappointment in self, others, and life circumstances. It may be worth your time to sit down and write out the significant experiences in your past as well as the shaping features of your current life situation in an attempt to better understand your own abilities to cope with stress.

As suggested in the previous paragraph, socio-economic status plays a big role in one's ability to cope with stress in a healthy way. There is a clear relationship between poverty and stress-related illness. The fewer resources one has, the more likely one is to develop an anxiety disorder or depression or another, maybe more severe, mental health disorder. Just as the brain is highly complex, so is the concept of socio-economic status. Financial stress, neighborhood safety, excessive work and lack of sleep, poor nutrition, and limited access to good health care all likely play a role in this phenomenon.

The way you and I respond to stress, the ways in which we protect ourselves or try to prevent an unhealthy response to stress, is influenced by countless factors. These factors – genetics, learned behaviors, past successes and failures, current life situation, and innumerable others yet to be defined – conspire to lead us to automatic responses to stressful events. The good news is that "automatic" does not mean "cannot be changed." We are not predestined by any of these factors, not even genetics. As we've seen in the chapters of this book, we can indeed, with help, break free from unhealthy learned and programmed patterns of stress responses and forge new, healthy ones.

Attitude is everything.

Possibly the most important factor in how we respond to stressors is how we *think* about them. That sounds a little hokey, but it's absolutely true. If we believe that the stressor is more than we can handle, we are not likely to handle it very well. If we believe that we don't have what it takes to deal with the stressor, we will not deal with it well.

Let's consider an example. For years, Mark has watched cancer attack his old high school buddies. One by one, it seems, all of his friends, the Gang, announced on Facebook or through a group email that they were battling one form of cancer or another: skin cancer, leukemia, colon cancer. From behind the barrier of his computer screen, he has peered into their lives as they first received the diagnosis. He has felt the sting of their initial shock, the sadness of the prospect of saying goodbye to friends and family, and the fear of the unknown days and weeks ahead. He watched helplessly as they physically transformed in front of his very eyes on the computer screen, first losing weight, then losing all of their hair. The pictures of these men, guys he used to play football with and had Guys' Wing Nights at the sports pub with, as they changed, became hardly recognizable. Years were added to their faces as the unavoidable wear and tear of stress, fear, depression, radiation, and chemotherapy took their toll on once youthful bodies and minds.

When news came that the best man in Mark's wedding had finally succumbed to his disease, Mark was devastated. He was filled with sadness, anger, fear – seemingly all at once. It didn't seem fair. He was too young, barely 60, and it felt like just yesterday that he and his pals had been learning to drive and asking girls out on first dates. Could this be how it ended for everyone? What was the point of it all, if death came so quickly, so early, and with such cruelty? What had been the meaning of it all if there was nothing more to hope for, no more big plans and dreams for the future? Mark sunk into a deep depression as he struggled to find answers to unanswerable questions.

In the months that followed, the initial pain subsided and was replaced with a low-level sadness, just barely perceptible, hovering in the background. When Mark thought about the death of his friend and the ongoing struggles of his other friends, he thanked God it wasn't him. He just knew that he couldn't handle going through what he was watching his friends go through. He wasn't made like them, he didn't have the faith and fortitude to struggle well in the face of losing odds. He'd rather just die, he told himself, than fight a losing battle for months, months of pain and sickness, months of fear and untold depression.

Then came that fateful doctor visit. When his family physician told him that he was worried that Mark might have cancer, and that he wanted him to see a specialist in the oncology department, Mark was devastated. It felt like an actual kick in the gut. He buckled over in agony, unable to breathe, unable to think clearly. After stumbling out of the clinic that day, Mark was never the same again. He walked through life like a zombie, unresponsive, uninterested, disengaged from everything and everyone. His wife tried to stay connected to him, but it was no use. He had checked out, given up. He felt hopeless and became helpless. He stopped bathing and taking care of himself. He quit attending their Wednesday night couples' Bible study. He lost interest in everything. What's the point? What was the point of everything if this was how it was always going to end?

You see what happened, don't you? Mark had set himself up to believe that life-threatening stressors meant the end of all meaning and purpose, and that he couldn't handle facing such a stressor. Stress is often the beginning of anxiety and depression. It's essential that we recall that the stress response begins with how we *think about* the stressors we're facing and our personal resources for coping with them. Remember General Beringer from War Games? His job was to take in all the information available and determine a DEFCON level based on his memories, experiences, training, and thoughts about the nature of the threat and his faith in the United States' military's capacity to handle it. While the amygdala, your personal General Beringer, likes to make use of your automatic thoughts as much as possible in order to make a quick decision and induce a quick response, you can in fact influence and even learn to override those automatic thoughts, and over time you can change your automatic thoughts by replacing them with more helpful, more truthful and accurate thoughts.

How might Mark's situation have been different if he had made a conscious attempt to form accurate and helpful thoughts about his friends' illnesses and death? How might his own experience with a cancer diagnosis been different if he had viewed the diagnosis differently, as a normal part of life on this earth, something by no means beyond the reach of a loving, caring God? What if he had been more confident in his own ability to cope with the unknown future?

Summing it all up

This has admittedly been a complicated chapter, and in many ways, it has actually been an *oversimplification* of the stress response! Let's take a couple minutes to sum up what we have learned.

The stress response is often the starting point for our mental and emotional struggles. Understanding it can alleviate fear and make us more self-compassionate about what we are going through. Beginning with the amygdala, the brain processes stressful information in light of our memories and beliefs, making a decision about the intensity of the threat, what we are calling our DEFCON level. If it decides that we need to adjust the DEFCON level, it does so by initiating two pathways. The slow path makes use of chemical signals called hormones, the most important of which is cortisol. The faster pathway relies on electrical signals through nerves that ultimately cause the release of epinephrine in the bloodstream and norepinephrine directly in the muscles and organs, including the brain. All of these chemicals bring the many changes we think of as the fight-or-flight response: dry mouth, racing and pounding heart, rapid and shallow breathing, upset stomach, fatigue, and so on. The purpose of these changes is to prepare us to do whatever it takes to survive a short-term physical threat on our lives. When the stressor is allowed to persist for long periods of time without resetting the system, or when we experience wave after wave of stressors without enough time to reset in between, the life-saving response begins to make us sick. This is especially true, for some reason, when the stressors are psychological in nature rather than physical. The good news in all of this is that, since the response begins with how we mentally process stressors and our own coping skills, we have the opportunity to change the outcome by learning to assess our situation accurately, by training ourselves in healthy coping skills, and by learning to trust our own capacity for dealing with anything life can throw at us.

The human being is an incredible creation. Not surprisingly, we are designed to handle incredible stressors, life-threatening stressors beyond anything most of us will ever experience. But we are only supposed to face them in short bursts, for minutes or hours at the most, followed by ample time to reset the system back to baseline levels again. When the stressors pile up, one after the other, and when they are messing not only with our physical health but also our mental well-being, the system becomes overloaded and we crash.

Appendix B

The Science of Psychiatric Medications

One step in the process that slowed down my recovery was finding the right medication. I know that some of my readers will object to the use of psychoactive medications.

- "What do we really know about how these medications affect our brains?"
- "You're just playing God with those drugs."
- "You need to believe in the power of prayer, not drugs."

Yes, by all means, pray without ceasing! As a scientist, though, I see nothing wrong with treating the brain like any other organ that has gone haywire. If my liver had a quiver, I'd see a liverologist and gladly take medications to fix the problem. When bacteria colonize my sinus cavity every couple of years, I am grateful for antibiotics like Z-Pak. While we do indeed need to take great care with the brain, it is still just an organ of the body, not a crystal ball or a magic box.

I think where we go wrong sometimes is that we mistake our brain for our soul, but the brain is no more equivalent to the soul than the pinky toe is. Your brain is made up of the same four primary building blocks of all tissue in your body: carbohydrates, proteins, lipids, and nucleic acids (DNA and RNA). These take shape to form specialized cells called neurons and glial cells whose functions are to communicate with one another, sort of a central clearinghouse for processing information to keep the body running and make decisions. It stands to reason, then, that when we medically treat the brain with surgery or chemical medications, we are not altering the soul or "playing God."

You and I are neither God nor a psychiatrist. So, let's all agree to quit shaming people who are approaching their mental health struggles in a different way than we think they should. When we do this, we are overstepping our qualification and doing more harm to them than good. While we might be justified in giving advice in the earliest stages of someone's emotional health struggles, once he or she is under the care of a mental health professional, our role changes to that of supporter, empathizer, and cheerleader, not doctor, therapist, or junior Holy Spirit.

Psychiatrists are MDs that can prescribe medications, while psychologists, counselors, and therapists are mental health professionals that take a psychological – non-medical – approach to helping us. When I finally got to see a psychiatrist, he started me with Prozac, probably the most common anti-anxiety/depression medication on the market today. Prozac (a.k.a. fluoxetine) is in a class of antidepressants called selective serotonin reuptake inhibitors (SSRIs). Serotonin is a neurotransmitter, a type of signal within the brain, that is involved in regulating our moods, among other functions. When specialized brain cells secrete serotonin, other cells can detect it and respond by creating a more positive mood. Serotonin that is not immediately detected by other cells can be taken up again by the same cells that secreted it in the first place. The purpose of Prozac and other SSRIs, then, is to inhibit this reuptake of serotonin, leaving it "out there" to be detected by other cells for a longer period of time. The effect is to reduce the effects of depression and anxiety.

It's important to understand that SSRIs are mood stabilizers, not mood lifters. In other words, there is no "high" from taking Prozac, no matter how much you take. The SSRIs are not the "happy drugs" depicted in movies that make you feel good even when life is going poorly. Instead, the SSRIs give your brain a chance to feel normal levels of happiness and peace. They just level the playing field when it feels like the anxiety and depression have an unfair advantage.

We do have to be careful when we tinker with an organ as complicated as the brain. For reasons unknown, SSRIs can sometimes actually *cause* deep depression, especially in younger patients. In my case, the first dose of Prozac coincided with a panic attack that lasted several hours. Ann took me into urgent care and the doctor there took me off the Prozac until I could see my psychiatrist again. My normal psych doctor didn't have any openings for more than a week, so I was scheduled to see another psychiatrist in the same office for a so-called "bridge appointment," a stop-gap measure to make sure I transitioned in a safe way from the hospital environment (in my case, urgent care) to outpatient care at home. This doctor was the first in my journey to really take notice of the urgency of my situation and offered to put me on a short-term intervention drug called Klonopin.

Also known generically as clonazepam, Klonopin falls into the benzodiazepine class of drugs. Benzos include the famously abused drug Valium, and all forms have essentially the same calming effects as Valium. Klonopin and Valium, like other benzos, work by enhancing the effects of a natural neurotransmitter called GABA (gamma-aminobutyric acid). GABA's primary function in adults is to calm and dampen brain activity – in other words, it's a sedative. Natural GABA plus a benzo drug combine to decrease the excitability of brain neurons. When we realize that anxiety and panic attacks are the result of brain cells shooting off like Fourth of July fireworks, it is easy to see how drugs like Klonopin can break the pattern.

As a scientist, I saw this as an experiment – I know it's nerdy, but it's how I think, and it allowed me to be a little more objective about my own case. You see, I still held onto some doubts about the diagnosis of anxiety and depression, and somewhere in the back of my mind I still wondered if we had missed some medical cause of my symptoms like cancer or maybe an endocrine disorder. Since Klonopin acts on brain cells to settle them down by enhancing GABA activity, it wouldn't be expected to have any effect at all on my symptoms if in fact they were caused by a tumor or faulty adrenal glands.

To interpret the results of this experiment, we should first remind ourselves of my health up to this point. For two months I had been experiencing steadily worsening gastrointestinal problems (nausea and diarrhea), vertigo, body aches, and general flu-like symptoms. My appetite was nil, and I had been growing weaker with each passing day. Throughout this time period I hadn't had more than a few of hours of relief from these symptoms.

Enter Klonopin, what a scientist might call the independent variable. Keeping all other variables the same (eating and sleeping patterns, other meds, etc.), we introduced a single change to the system. The hope, then, was that any change in symptoms (the dependent variables) would be attributable to the Klonopin, the one thing we tweaked. If this were a true drug testing experiment (called a clinical trial), we'd have hundreds or thousands of replicates, other people suffering from similar symptoms taking the medications as well. My experiment wasn't a clinical trial, though, so it was just me. Not perfect, but it would have to do.

If the doctors' hypothesis was correct, that I was suffering from anxiety and depression, then we could predict the outcome of the experiment: my symptoms would be alleviated with the Klonopin. And that's exactly what happened. Quickly. Within just a few hours the body aches and vertigo all but disappeared. I felt like I could get up and get around again as some strength returned to my body, and I was hungry again. For the first time in weeks I was really *hungry*. It was like letting out a huge sigh of relief. The diagnosis, it appeared, was accurate and I was finally on track to healing. A strange, unfamiliar feeling crept in: hope. For the first time on this journey, I was truly hopeful of this ship turning around and getting my life back.

Klonopin gets a bad rap, though, and it may be well deserved. When used in high doses or in low doses for more than a couple of weeks it can be addictive. Admittedly, I began looking forward to my daily dose of the chill pill. By dulling my brain's communication network, not only did my hyper-sensitive anxiety settle down, most worries faded in their importance. I could breathe deeply again, relax again, and smile again. *One of the kids got in trouble at school today? Bummer. We're overdrawn on our checking account? Oh well.* Best of all, I felt well enough to eat and leave the house again. The benzos are indeed "happy pills," and I was very eager for my happy dose each day.

For his part, my regular psychiatrist wasn't pleased with the urgent care doc undoing his Prozac prescription. "How do you know the Prozac caused the panic attack?" he asked me in his office a few days later.

"I don't," I replied.

He nodded and smiled. "Well, let's try something different."

I had been having almost daily panic attacks without any medication, so who was to say that the Prozac caused this latest attack? A fundamental principle of science and medicine says that *correlation does not prove causation*. Whatever had been causing my panic attacks may have still been at work and may have been responsible for this latest episode. For that matter, the simple *thought* of taking my first psychoactive medication – especially in the fragile mental state I was in – may have been enough to set off panic. My psychiatrist switched me to Lexapro, another SSRI related to Prozac, in the hopes that I would tolerate it better. No panic this time, and no apparent side effects.

I was fortunate to have found a medication that I could tolerate so quickly. I have met many people who have struggled for years to find the right medications to control their anxiety or depression, often with miserable side effects. The only advice I can give is to stick with it and not give up. You may have had a bad experience or two with medications, but I bet there is something out there that can help you to overcome your struggles, something that can bring just enough calm to your mind for you to be able to think clearly and begin working on lifelong strategies for building resilience against attack. I don't view medications as the final solution, but sometimes, for some people, they can help bring the clarity needed to allow you to begin working on those long-term solutions.

If my psychiatrist was frustrated with the urgent care doctor for telling me to quit taking Prozac, he was even less pleased with the psych doctor I saw at my bridge appointment who put me on Klonopin. He was aware of its addictive nature and the latest research was showing possible severe side effects including decreased cognitive function – feeling less "sharp" – and impaired short-term memory. But I had been taking it daily for nearly a month by this time, so quitting "cold turkey" was not an option.

I was taking 2 mg per day, so he started by decreasing my dose to 1.5 mg, a 25% decrease. It was miserable. I felt sick, panicky, agitated. It reminded me of the horrible hangovers I used to get after partying in Tijuana when I was eighteen with the added bonus of sitting on the edge of panic. Mostly I just felt like I needed more Klonopin. Day two was a little better and by day three I felt like I could function again. After a week I repeated the cycle: drop 0.5 mg, lie in bed curled up like a baby, wishing it would all go away. Two more step-downs and I was done with Klonopin, hopefully once and for all. It was a lifesaver in the midst of the storm, but it was a beast to quit.

Again, I was fortunate with how well I tolerated Klonopin. I've read and personally heard many nightmare stories about Klonopin addiction, side effects, and withdrawal that make my experience seem like a day at the county fair. Singer Stevie Nicks has famously blamed Klonopin for taking her into "hell" and essentially ruining her life. She was prescribed the drug during detox from cocaine, a common application of benzos. Unfortunately, many people discover they have only traded one addiction for another in the process.

My experience with Klonopin highlights an important point in the recovery journey: even though we all share many common experiences, my mess is uniquely my own, therefore my recovery will necessarily be uniquely my own. My particular combination of childhood experiences, genetic constitution, habits and hangups, choices I have made and choices that have been made for me, love and support (or lack of), stressors and pleasures, all conspire to create a situation that is distinctly my own. It comes as no surprise, then, that the way out of my situation will not be exactly the same as anyone else's way out of their own troubles. A medication that worked for me may not be right for you. A particularly themed support group might be a waste of time for me even though it turned your life around completely. Remember, there's no place for being judgmental of others on their journey to wellness.

Klonopin interrupted the hellish panic attacks by increasing the natural calming effects of GABA. Lexapro stabilized my serotonin levels. Weekly talk therapy sessions helped me to begin to understand what was going on and how I got there. The downward spiral seemed to have stopped, and a slight upward trajectory had become barely perceptible. Four months after the diagnosis of generalized anxiety disorder and depression, I returned to my work at the University, albeit at a reduced teaching load.

As I sit in my local coffee shop today, recounting these stories, it has been almost four years since the diagnosis. People ask me how I'm doing, if I'm back to 100% again. I don't think that's the right question. One thing I've learned along this journey is that I was never 100% to begin with. In fact, I don't think any of us is operating at 100%. In some ways, maybe I'm at 110% now, because now I understand myself so much better. I understand my stressors and my go-to responses. I have tools for preventing disproportionate responses, and other tools to deal with stress, anxiety, or depression when they hit. And they do still hit. I'm human, and life is difficult at times.

Do I still have stressful days? Absolutely. Do I still have times of inexplicable anxiety or sadness? You bet. Jesus promised us trials in this life. He also promised that He'd be right by our side during those trials, and that He'd use them for our own good and the good of His kingdom. Amen.

So, don't be discouraged if it takes longer for you to heal from your anxiety or depression than it did to heal from the leg you broke skiing or that nasty sinus infection you just beat. And don't be surprised when your solutions don't look like your mom's solutions or the solutions some guy told you about in a book. Time, persistence, a desire to recover, and a willingness to seek (and follow) professional help. Be patient. Pray. Don't give up.

Finally, always bear in mind that psychoactive drugs are not something to trifle with. It is unwise and unsafe to start and stop taking these kinds of medications without your doctor's oversight. Just like self-diagnosis is dangerous business, you also don't want to increase or decrease your dosage without your doctor's instructions. Medications can stop working, or they may need adjustments from time to time, so stay in close contact with your psychiatrist.

Common anxiety and depression medications

You might find it helpful to learn a little more about the most common medicines used to treat and prevent anxiety and depression. This is not meant to serve as a prescription for anyone, just information to help you understand your own medications or to give you a common language for discussing medication options with your doctor. Remember, self-diagnosis can be dangerous, and self-prescription is even more dangerous!

MAOIs. The monoamine oxidase inhibitors were the first medications developed for anxiety, panic, social phobia, and depression. Monoamine oxidases (MAOs) are enzymes in the brain that degrade serotonin, norepinephrine, and dopamine. MAO inhibitors, then, block this degradation and allow these three key neurotransmitters to accumulate. When we consider that all three are involved in generating a sense of calm in the mind, it makes sense that the MAOIs would induce calm in an anxious or depressed person. Unfortunately, the MAOIs come with some pretty miserable side effects for many people, so they have been largely replaced by more recently developed drugs that are generally safer. The MAOIs still have an important place, though, particularly for people whose anxiety or depression doesn't respond well to the more common medications in use. Only four are currently approved by the FDA for treating depression in particular: isocarboxazid (Marplan), phenelzine (Nardil), selegiline (Emsam), and tranylcypromine (Parnate).

Tricyclics. Cyclic antidepressants (commonly called tricyclics) block the reuptake of the neurotransmitters serotonin and norepinephrine, both of which help regulate mood and DEFCON level. By blocking reuptake, serotonin and norepinephrine accumulate and help stabilize your emotions and enable you to think more clearly. Like the MAOIs, tricyclics can effectively treat anxiety as well as depression, but also like the MAOIs, tricyclics can cause some uncomfortable and even dangerous side effects so they are being used less often in favor of newer drugs. There are numerous tricyclics in use today, but the most common ones include amitriptyline (Elavil), imipramine (Tofranil), and nortriptyline (Pamelor).

Benzodiazepines. As discussed earlier, benzos are GABA-enhancing drugs that act by improving the ability of naturally occurring GABA produced in your brain to bind to its receptors. Remember that GABA is like the brakes of your nervous system, slowing things down, calming the mind and nerves. Enhancing GABA's ability to bind to its receptors increases its calming effects. Benzos have often been abused and must be used with extreme caution since they can be addictive. Clonazepam (Klonopin), diazepam (Valium), lorazepam (Ativan), and alprazolam (Xanax) are among the most common benzos in use today.

SSRIs. The selective serotonin reuptake inhibitors (SSRIs) are the most commonly prescribed medications for both anxiety and depression in the world today. They can be very effective, are slow-acting and therefore less likely to be abused, have few side effects for most people, and are generally non-addictive. As the name

205

implies, they work by inhibiting the reuptake of the neurotransmitter serotonin, increasing its levels in the brain and enhancing its calming and mood-stabilizing effects. Unlike the benzos, which act within minutes, the SSRIs require many weeks before any noticeable effects can be seen. Some SSRIs you may have seen include fluoxetine (Prozac), escitalopram (Lexapro), citalopram (Celexa), paroxetine (Paxil), and sertraline (Zoloft).

SNRIs. A close relative of the SSRI class are the SNRIs, or serotonin and norepinephrine reuptake inhibitors. By increasing levels of both neurotransmitters in the brain, they cooperate to increase calm, decrease depression, and regulate mood and emotions. Four SNRIs are currently approved by the FDA: duloxetine (Cymbalta), desvenlafaxine (Pristiq), levomilnacipran (Fetzima), and venlafaxine (Effexor). SNRIs have also been used to control chronic nerve pain.

Beta blockers. Beta blockers are a class of anxiolytic (anxiety-stopping) medications that act on your heart to slow its rate and decrease its pumping force. Like we learned in an earlier chapter about how slow, deep breathing sends a message to the brain that all is well and the DEFCON level can be lowered again, beta blockers decrease heart rate and pumping force, sending a message to the brain that the world is safe at the moment and the stress response can be switched off again. They are also useful for treating heart disorders (*e.g.*, high blood pressure), migraines, and tremors. The most commonly prescribed beta blockers include propranolol (Inderal) and metoprolol (Lopressor). As an example of the use of a beta blocker, I sometimes take propranolol for my flying anxiety. While it does not take away the phobia entirely, my body responds to turbulence less dramatically when I use it.

I want to make a few final comments about medications before we leave this subject. It can be downright scary listening to a narrator work down a long list of possible side effects of a drug on a TV commercial. More than once people have said to me, "Why would I want to take this medication and trade the one problem I have for all of these horrible side effects?" The advertisements sure do make it sound like you are taking your life into your own hands if you decide to take a particular drug. In some ways, you are.

It's all about risk assessment. We do it every day without thinking about it.

- "Is it worth getting in my car and driving the freeway to work? I could get into an accident. I could be killed."
- "Is it worth eating the leftover Chinese food I put in the fridge on Tuesday? What if it has spoiled and I spend the next 24 hours in the bathroom?"
- "Is it worth marrying this person I love? What if she decides later that I'm not the right man for her? She could break my heart."
- "Is it worth swimming in the ocean at the beach? There could be sharks."

Every single day we make decisions that involve risk assessment, and managing our health is no different. There are no medical procedures or medications that are risk-free. But the beauty of clinical trials is that at least we know the risks before we begin taking a medication. You have to understand that a medicine has to go through many years of testing for the FDA to give its approval for human use. The process goes something like this:

After many years of development and testing in the laboratory, including testing the drug's effects on live animals, the FDA may give approval for the drug to be tested on a small number of people (fewer than one hundred). If all goes well in these phase-1 clinical trials, approval may be granted to increase the number of test subjects to several hundred (phase 2). In phase 3, upwards of a few thousand people are tested for their reactions to the drug under investigation. Through all these trials, every adverse reaction is carefully described and reported to the FDA. This is how that long list of possible side effects reported in the magazine and television ads is created. And every single side effect has to be noted and reported, even if only one person in three thousand showed this effect. If the FDA finds the risk to be acceptable (remember, there is no such thing as zero-risk health care), it assigns a committee to do a thorough review of everything the drug company (called the sponsor) has done and learned in the past several years about their proposed medication. Only about 8% of the proposed drugs that begin the process with the FDA make it to market, and that typically takes ten or more years and averages close to $100 million in research and development costs for the sponsor. (This is a large reason why prescription costs are so high – the drug company's main motivation is to run a successful business, and that means recuperating costs and making a profit. It's hard to blame them for that.)

The next time your doctor recommends a particular medication for your mental health condition, carefully consider the known risks of taking the drug, and weigh them honestly against the risks of *not* taking the drug. Keep in mind that the drug was rigorously tested in thousands of people before it hit the market. If it is not a new drug, then tens of thousands, maybe hundreds of thousands or even millions of people have since used this medication, and many of their responses have been reported as well. Weigh the risks and make the decision based on evidence rather than fear or a gut feeling. Don't forget that your doctor is on your side and can help you with this process.

Taking medication to balance your serotonin levels is no more "playing God" than taking an antibiotic for a urinary tract infection. Even if you're still not convinced that medications might be an acceptable piece to the puzzle of mental and emotional health care, don't pretend to be a doctor and tell other people what their approach should be to medications. Shame has no place in this process. There are a variety of medications in use today to assist people with their anxiety and depression struggles, each of them acting to bring calm to an agitated mind in one way or another by altering levels of key neurotransmitters in the brain. Each of these drugs has gone through years of research, development, and rigorous testing before coming to the market, and although the possible side effects may seem daunting, you have the ability to make an educated decision *based*

on the evidence as to whether you can accept the risks of a particular medication.

Appendix C

The Serenity Prayer, Reinhold Niebuhr (1892-1971)

God, grant me the serenity to accept the things I cannot change,
the courage to change the things I can,
and the wisdom to know the difference,
living one day at a time,
enjoying one moment at a time,
accepting hardship as a pathway to peace,
taking, as Jesus did, this sinful world as it is, not as I would have it,
trusting that You will make all things right if I surrender to Your will,
so that I may be reasonably happy in this life,
and supremely happy with You forever in the next.
Amen.

Appendix D

Dave's Testimony

I was born and raised in the 1970s and 1980s amid the rolling hills and hardwood forests of western New York. We camped, fished, and hiked during three out of four seasons, and the sights and smells of the eastern woodlands became more comfortable than those of the cities. When I wasn't out in the fields and streams, I was reading Field and Stream Magazine, daydreaming about catching a trophy trout or spotting the biggest buck in the herd across a snowy field. Times were different then. My friends and I would stay out riding bikes and running around the neighborhood until dark, and my parents, as far as I know, didn't worry much about us. Empty fields and wooded lots were important tutors and set me up for a lifetime drawn to nature and the kinds of adventures that are only found far from the concrete and exhaust of the city.

Overall, I had a happy childhood, although my parents divorced when I was five years old, bringing with it a set of emotional challenges. My brother TC dealt with it head on with confrontation and rebellion, while I tried to be the peacemaker. I just wanted everything to be OK, even if I had to fake it. Otherwise, we did what kids do: went to school, did our homework (sometimes), hung out with friends, and tried to grow up. Nothing too out of the ordinary.

TC and I had, and still have, a great relationship. He's almost three years older and at least four inches taller. He beat me up often. I usually deserved it. I was good, though, at getting him in trouble for it. We had a sort of understanding: I'd push his buttons, he'd haul off and give me a thumping, I'd holler louder than was necessary, and he'd get scolded. Same story for brothers going back countless generations, probably all the way to Cain and Abel. Nothing new under the sun.

We were not a church-going family, except at Christmas and Easter some years, but there was a general morality that pervaded our home. I can remember visiting a local church and attending Sunday school classes with other kids. I even participated in a children's choir at one church we attended for a couple of months. Beyond that, I figured God must be out there somewhere, but who He was or what He wanted from me was a mystery.

When I was twelve, TC and I changed cities to live with my father and his new wife and a new baby sister, Aimee. They lived in a rough part of town, so my brother and I were enrolled at the local Catholic schools, not for reasons of religious training but for safety reasons and the high-quality educational opportunities. My junior high school was run by nuns while the high school was operated by Jesuit priests. Sister Anne used to scold me for using the Italian profanities my Paisano friends taught me. I just played dumb. The Jesuit priests were a hoot. It was an all-boys school to eliminate the social pressures of talking to girls. All it really did, though, was bring out the worst in our language and hygiene. You should have been a fly on the wall during Father O'Malley's sex ed class!

Being non-Catholic, I was a little bit of an outsider, though no one ever made me feel that way. Religion classes focused on Catholic history and uniquely Catholic doctrines such as Mary's immaculate conception or the importance of praying to the saints for help. Probably owing more to my own lack of interest rather than any neglect on the part of my educators, I never really learned much about my sinful state or my need for a savior. It never occurred to me to read the Bible or even to pray on my own, so I never felt that I knew God any better than before I attended Catholic schools. But my experiences in the parochial school system did further solidify my sense that God was real and that He was good, though I could not have told you much about Him beyond that.

When we graduated from high school, all of my friends were heading off to excellent colleges like Notre Dame, La Salle, and Canisius. I wasn't feeling particularly inspired, though, and had no idea what I wanted to do with my life. I half-heartedly looked into Iowa State University (my dad's alma mater) and Purdue (I was a Boilermaker football fan in those days), but in the end, the only thing I knew I was ready for was a change.

TC had joined the Navy a couple years before and was stationed in San Diego with Seal Team Three. I had visited a couple of times and fallen in love with the place, so when I graduated from high school and needed a change of scenery, San Diego was an obvious choice. Two short weeks after receiving my diploma, my friend Brian and I rented half of a moving truck and drove 2,663 miles southwest in pursuit of the California dream. We spent the first few days after arriving in the Golden State sleeping in the back of the moving truck until we found a place to rent for a few weeks while we looked for something at the beach.

We both landed dead-end jobs that barely paid the rent and immediately jumped into the party scene. I got a fake ID and starting testing it out at all the local bars and liquor stores. I looked twelve but was trying to pass for twenty-five, but where there is a will there is a way, and I found plenty of people to party with. Before long I was hanging out with a crowd that, like me, just wanted to have fun. We were drinking, smoking dope, and using progressively stronger drugs at least four or five nights a week. I was living the dream, so I thought.

Part of the deception of alcohol and drugs was the illusion that I could handle it. *I can quit anytime I want*, I would tell myself. *I just don't want to right now.* Somehow my self-image and sense of self-worth had gotten wrapped up in this image of the party guy. If I was home on a Wednesday night watching TV, I must be some sort of loser. Eventually I found myself going to bars alone if none of my friends were available, and not long after that I got lazy and just started drinking alone at home. So much for my "social drinker" excuse. More than once I tried to quit only to be drawn back to the bottle within a few days. I don't think it was biological addiction – I never experienced the physiological effects of withdrawal. But I was clearly psychologically addicted.

Another deception of this lifestyle is that there is no other life option, no other way to live and be happy, at least not for me. All of my friends were part of this party scene, and it was my primary social activity. Who was I if not a party guy? Who were my friends if not these party friends?

In the midst of all this wild living, I somehow had the sense to realize that I needed to go to college. Maybe it was the $4.25/hour minimum wage I was earning as a busboy. Or maybe I saw that I didn't want to still be living this way when I was an adult. Either way, I started taking classes at the local community college while I tried to figure out what I wanted to be when I grew up. After two and

213

a half years, though, they told me it was time to go to a four-year school – there were no more classes I could take that would transfer towards a college degree. I had a decision to make. Do I go to one of the huge state schools, with tens of thousands of students and classes of three hundred or more? Do I maybe try the Catholic college? After all, I was already familiar enough with Catholicism to not be too surprised. Honestly, though, I wasn't in too much of a hurry for more nuns and priests, so I steered clear. Then a young woman I worked with mentioned a small private school on the beach that might suit me, but I would have to go to chapel and take Bible classes.

I enrolled at Point Loma Nazarene College in San Diego as a twenty-one-year old transfer student, coming in after two and a half years in the community college system. Not only was I not a Christian, I was openly antagonistic towards people who spoke of Jesus in the present tense or talked about the Bible as if it was anything more than a book of historical fiction. I thought they were simplistic, naive, gullible. I assumed they must be weak and needy, so a faith in God made them feel better. I ascribed more to the philosophy of Esqueleto in Nacho Libre (to be read with a really exaggerated Mexican accent): "I don't know why you always have to be judging me because I only believe in science!"[1]

It was something of a marvel that I willingly enrolled at an evangelical college, paying private college tuition, surrounded by "blind faith" Christians, and required to take Bible classes and attend chapel, which I often skipped. When I did attend chapel, I sat in the back of the auditorium, a cassette tape in my Sony Walkman playing Nirvana or AC/DC, headphones on to silence the sound of worship and preaching. I was an English major in those days, so I always had stacks of reading to do. Chapel was more of a study hall than a time of spiritual growth. Instead of "Lord I Lift Your Name on High" and a message on Ephesians 2:10, it was "Hells Bells" and *The Road Not Taken* for me.

I think somehow those chapel messages were leaking past my headphones and into my brain, though. I tried to resist the message I was hearing every day and seeing lived out in the lives of the students around me, but it eventually became irresistible. I started asking questions.

- *How do you know the Bible is God's Word and can actually be trusted?*
- *What makes you so sure Jesus wasn't just a good teacher?*
- *Do you really believe that all those miracles happened, and that Jesus even rose from the dead?*
- *What about all the other world religions? How can they all be wrong?*

It's interesting to me to recall how my Christian friends at PLNC didn't have all the answers to my questions, and didn't even pretend to, for that matter. They explained what they could, expressed their hope in Jesus the best they could, pointed me to the Bible and prayer as often as possible to answer my questions, and said "I don't know" in just about every conversation. So often we fear sharing our faith because we think we will be outsmarted by someone, that we won't be able to answer all of their questions. My experience suggests that having all the answers is not necessary to share our faith with other people. What matters is honesty, expressing the hope that we have (1 Peter 3:15) and why we cling to it, admitting our doubts and confessing what we do not understand. The world isn't looking for a bullet-proof faith within the church before it will believe. The world just wants to know that they can follow Jesus and still be human.

During Christmas break of my final year, I gave my life to Christ at a small worship service on campus. I truly prayed for the first time since my childhood, asking God to reveal Himself to me if He was real. During that prayer, my heart was convicted of pride – I had put up walls between God and me because I didn't want to change, I didn't want to admit that I wasn't in charge and that I didn't have all the answers.

I left that worship service humbled and ready to listen, ready to learn. I began attending church services – Catholic mass, tiny Baptist services, mega-church productions – anything I thought would draw me closer to God. I continued to ask tough questions of my Christian friends, but now I was actually wanting to learn the answers rather than trying to stump them or prove my position. I learned during this time that I didn't have to have all of the answers to my questions before choosing to follow after God. I learned that I didn't have to have it all together before becoming a Christian. I discovered, to use

Brennan Manning's words, that "getting honest with ourselves does not make us unacceptable to God."[2] I could be filled with doubts and questions, and God would find me acceptable nonetheless as I sought to know Him.

It has been an amazing twenty-four years, and I'm left breathless thinking about all that the future holds!

Notes

Chapter 1. A Bear in My Camp
[1] Louv, Richard. *The Nature Principle: Reconnecting with Life in a Virtual Age*. Chapel Hill: Algonquin Books, 2012.

Chapter 2. A Bear in My Life
[1] Lewis, C. S. *A Grief Observed*. New York: HarperOne, 1961.

Chapter 4. The *Real* Doctors
[1] Brand, Paul, and Philip Yancey. *The Gift of Pain: Why We Hurt and What We Can Do about It*. Grand Rapids: Zondervan, 1997.
[2] Adams, Susan. "The Least Stressful Jobs of 2013," Forbes, January 3, 2013. https://www.forbes.com/sites/susanadams/2013/01/03/the-least-stressful-jobs-of-2013/#1208cae16e24
[3] Eagen, Kevin et. al. *Undergraduate Teaching Faculty: The 2013-2014 HERI Faculty Survey*. Los Angeles: Higher Education Research Institute, UCLA, 2014. https://www.heri.ucla.edu/monographs/HERI-FAC2014-monograph-expanded.pdf

Chapter 5. Not Alone
[1] Weir, Andy. *The Martian*. New York: Penguin Random House, 2014.
[2] Data from the US Centers for Disease Control and Prevention (CDC), the National Institute of Mental Health (NIMH), the National Alliance on Mental Illness (NAMI), and the American Foundation for Suicide Prevention (AFSP).
[3] Simpson, Amy. *Troubled Minds: Mental Illness and the Church's Mission*. Downer's Grove: IVP Books, 2013.
[4] Data from the National Institute of Mental Health (NIMH).
[5] Barna Group. *Barna Trends 2017: What's Next and What's New at the Intersection of Faith and Culture*. Grand Rapids: Baker Books, 2016.

[6] Barna Group. *The State of Pastors: How Today's Faith Leaders Are Navigating Life and Leadership in an Age of Complexity.* Barna Group, 2017.

[7] LifeWay Research. "Most Teenagers Drop Out of Church as Young Adults." January 15, 2019. https://lifewayresearch.com/2019/01/15/most-teenagers-drop-out-of-church-as-young-adults/

[8] Data from the National Institute of Mental Health (NIMH).

[9] Data from the Chronicle of Higher Education and the National Alliance on Mental Illness (NAMI).

[10] LifeWay Research. "Mental Illness Remains Taboo Topic for Many Pastors." September 22, 2014. https://lifewayresearch.com/2014/09/22/mental-illness-remains-taboo-topic-for-many-pastors/

Chapter 6. Sober Judgment

[1] Cloud, Henry, and John Townsend. *Boundaries: When to Say Yes, How to Say No to Take Control of Your Life.* Grand Rapids: Zondervan, 1992.

[2] The Serenity Prayer is attributed to Reinhold Niebuhr (1892-1971). You can find a common version of it in Appendix C.

Chapter 7. True or False

[1] Tripp, Paul David. *Lost in the Middle: Midlife and the Grace of God.* Wapwallopen: Shepherd Press, 2004.

[2] Brown, Brené. *Daring Greatly: How the Courage to Be Vulnerable Transforms the Way We Live, Love, Parent, and Lead.* New York: Avery, 2012.

[3] Thurman, Chris. *The Lies We Believe.* Nashville: Thomas Nelson, 2003.

Chapter 8. You Can Keep the Change

[1] Frost, Robert. "Nothing Gold Can Stay," from *Selected Poems of Robert Frost.* Orlando: Holt, Rinehart and Winston, Inc., 1963.

[2] Holmes, T. H., and R. H. Rahe, "The social readjustment rating scale," *Journal of Psychosomatic Research* (1967) 11, 213-218.

[3] Esipova, N. et al. "381 Million Adults Worldwide Migrate within Countries," Gallup (May 15, 2013).

[4] Friedman, Zack. "Student Loan Debt in 2017: A $1.3 Trillion Crisis," Forbes (February 21, 2017).

Chapter 9. Crazy Busy
[1] DeYoung, Kevin. *Crazy Busy: A (Mercifully) Short Book about a (Really) Big Problem*. Wheaton: Crossway, 2013.
[2] Texas A&M Transportation Institute. "Annual Study Shows Traffic Congestion Worsening in Cities Large and Small," September 18, 2007.
https://tti.tamu.edu/news/annual-study-shows-traffic-congestion-worsening-in-cities-large-and-small/
[3] Barna Group. "Tired & Stressed, but Satisfied: Moms Juggle Kids, Career & Identity," Barna Group, May 5, 2014.
https://www.barna.com/research/tired-stressed-but-satisfied-moms-juggle-kids-career-identity/
[4] Swenson, Richard A. *Margin: Restoring Emotional, Physical, Financial, and Time Reserves to Overloaded Lives*. Colorado Springs: NavPress, 1992.
[5] van der Kolk, Bessel. *The Body Keeps the Score: Brain, Mind, and Body in the Healing of Trauma*. New York: Penguin Books, 2014.

Chapter 10. Fighting Back
[1] Niequist, Shauna. *Present over Perfect: Leaving Behind Frantic for a Simpler, More Soulful Way of Living*. Grand Rapids: Zondervan, 2016.
[2] Swenson, Richard A. *Margin: Restoring Emotional, Physical, Financial, and Time Reserves to Overloaded Lives*. Colorado Springs: NavPress, 1992.
[3] Barna Group. *Barna Trends 2017: What's Next and What's New at the Intersection of Faith and Culture*. Grand Rapids: Baker Books, 2016.

Chapter 11. Great Expectations
[1] The Gin Blossoms, "Hey Jealousy" (on *Dusted*, Warner/Chappell Music, 1989).
[2] Tripp, Paul David. *Lost in the Middle: Midlife and the Grace of God*. Wapwallopen: Shepherd Press, 2004.

[3] Bruno, Dave. *The 100 Thing Challenge: How I Got Rid of Almost Everything, Remade my Life, and Regained my Soul*. New York: Harper, 2010.

[4] Porche, Brady. "Poll: 2 in 5 Americans Lose Sleep over Health Care Costs," creditcards.com, April 19, 2017. https://www.creditcards.com/credit-card-news/losing-sleep-money-worries-poll.php

[5] MacArthur Foundation, "How Housing Matters," www.macfound.org (April-May 2016).

[6] El Issa, Erin. "2016 American Household Credit Card Debt Study," nerdwallet.com, 2016. https://www.nerdwallet.com/blog/credit-card-data/household-credit-card-debt-study-2016/

[7] Gathergood, John. "Debt and Depression: Causal Links and Social Norm Effects," *The Economic Journal* (2012) 122, 1094-1114. https://onlinelibrary.wiley.com/doi/abs/10.1111/j.1468-0297.2012.02519.x

[8] American Psychological Association. "Stress in America: Paying with our Health," 2015. https://www.apa.org/news/press/releases/stress/2014/financial-stress

[9] American Psychological Association. "Stress in America: The State of our Nation," November 1, 2017. https://www.apa.org/images/state-nation_tcm7-225609.pdf

[10] Luskin, Fred. *Forgive for Good: A Proven Prescription for Health and Happiness*. New York: HarperOne, 2002.

[11] Young, Wm. Paul. *The Shack: Where Tragedy Confronts Eternity*. Newbury Park: Windblown Media, 2007.

[12] Fisher, Suzanne Woods. *Amish Peace: Simple Wisdom for a Complicated World*. Grand Rapids: Revell, 2009.

Chapter 12. The Resilience Workshop Part I

[1] American Psychological Association. https://www.apa.org/helpcenter/road-resilience

[2] Feder, A., D. Charney, and K. Collins. "Neurobiology of resilience" in *Resilience and Mental Health: Challenges Across the Lifespan* (eds. S. M. Southwick, B. T. Litz, D. Charney, and M. J. Friedman). Cambridge: Cambridge University Press, 2011.

[3] Bernard Meltzer (1916-1998)

[4] Thaler, Richard H., and Cass R. Sunstein. *Nudge: Improving Decisions about Health, Wealth, and Happiness.* New York: Penguin Books, 2009.

Chapter 13. The Resilience Workshop Part II
[1] Ratey, John. *Spark: The Revolutionary New Science of Exercise and the Brain.* New York: Little, Brown, and Company, 2008.
[2] Louv, Richard. *Last Child in the Woods: Saving our Children from Nature-Deficit Disorder.* Chapel Hill: Algonquin Books, 2008.

Chapter 14. More than Conquerors
[1] Brown, Brené. *Daring Greatly: How the Courage to Be Vulnerable Transforms the Way We Live, Love, Parent, and Lead.* New York: Avery, 2012.
[2] Frankl, Viktor. *Man's Search for Meaning.* Boston: Beacon Press, 1959.

Appendix D. Dave's Testimony
[1] Nacho Libre. Directed by Jared Hess. Paramount Pictures, 2006.
[2] Manning, B. *The Ragamuffin Gospel.* New York: Multnomah Books, 1999.

Made in the USA
San Bernardino, CA
24 April 2019